SECOND EDITION

CREATING HIGH PERFORMERS

7 QUESTIONS
TO ASK YOUR DIRECT REPORTS

WILLIAM DANN

FOREWORD BY KEN BLANCHARD
AUTHOR OF *THE NEW ONE MINUTE MANAGER*

Margie
Enjoy!
Ken

Creating High Performers:
7 Questions to Ask Your Direct Reports Published through Growth Press, LLC

Paperback ISBN: 978-0-99094-402-7

GROWTH PRESS

Growth Press, LLC 721 Depot Drive, Anchorage, AK 99501

Table of Contents

Foreword   v

Acknowledgments   vii

1. Introduction to Second Edition   1
2. The Role of Manager and Supervisor   5
3. The Two Types of Performance Problems   16
4. Why A Change in Role and Approach Matters   26
5. The 7 Questions   31

     Question #1 – Expectations   36

     Question #2 – Good Performance   43

     Question #3 – Feedback   47

     Question #4 – Authority   52

     Question #6 – Resources   59

     Question #7 – Credit   68

6. The Performance Context   74
7. Relationship and The Underlying Principle of Fairness   78
8. Putting the 7 Questions to Work   87
9. Identifying and Handling the "Won't Do" Employee   113
10. Troubleshooting   126
11. Some Final Thoughts   132

Appendix 1   135

Appendix 2   136

Appendix 3   139

Foreword

For a long time, I've been interested in the subject of managing people's performance. To me, there have always been three parts of that process: *performance planning*, where you set goals and establish coaching strategies; *day-to-day coaching*, where you follow through on what you agreed upon in order to help people win by accomplishing their goals; and *performance evaluation,* where you assess how well the person has performed over time. Of these three aspects, which typically is the most time consuming for managers? Performance evaluation. This tends to be the time when they have to sit down and fill out forms on each of their people and sort them into a normal distribution format. Only a few will win, a few have to lose, and the rest are considered average. Or, even worse, they may have to rank order their people. Bill Dann condemns this process, and so do I.

It has always amazed me how very few organizations do extensive performance planning where clear goals are set. They're even worse when it comes to how little day-to-day coaching goes on.

I always ask managers in my training sessions "How many of you hire losers? Do you say, 'We lost some of our best losers last year, so let's hire some new ones to fill those low spots'? Of course, you don't! You either hire winners—people who already have good performance records in their position; or you hire potential winners—people whom you believe you can train to be high performers. Obviously, you don't hire on a normal distribution curve."

Bill Dann and I wonder why every leader or manager wouldn't want every person to potentially win—to be a high performer who gets A's? Yet, to do that, managers have to talk to their people. That's why I love Bill's book. He introduces 7 questions you can use to partner with your people for better performance.

Peter Drucker always said, "Nothing good ever happens by accident." If you want something good to happen, you have to put some structure around it. If you want your people to perform well, meet and talk with them about how they are performing. Use Bill Dann's good questions and I guarantee not only that you will become a better leader/ manager, but that your people will become better performers.

This second edition adds a chapter on the distinction between supervisor and manager, expands on the role of managers and explains why that role needs to shift. Also added are in-depth guidance on how to introduce the 7 Questions method to employees, the importance of relationship, the multiple ways the 7 Questions can be used to fulfill a manager's role and an expanded treatment of how to deal with underperformers.

These changes all serve to provide managers greater clarity re. how to get employees to optimum performance and how to deal with those choosing not to go there.

Thanks Bill, you're the best.

Ken Blanchard, Co-Founder, The Ken Blanchard Companies

Author of *The New One Minute Manager*® *and Servant Leadership in Action*

Acknowledgments

It took a long while and lots of encouragement to bring about the first edition. Those who deserve to be credited include students of mine, co-workers, partners, clients, friends and loved ones. There are too many of you to mention again in this edition. But there are a few of you that I want acknowledge for their contribution to this second edition.

First, my friend and mentor, Ken Blanchard. In addition to being an inspiration as a human being, Ken taught me the meaning and essence of developing people. He has continued to encourage me to share my own learnings.

Second, I want to acknowledge John Gregoire, current owner and CEO of Professional Growth Systems, with whom I have collaborated on training and coaching to implement the 7 Questions in organizations. John shares my passion for work becoming the source for satisfaction and energy in our lives. He has an insight into the challenges of making the shift to a "coach" and to deploying the 7 Questions. His insights have been instrumental in the additions to this second edition. An expanded treatment of what has been learned to date, the impact on organizations and how to implement what we now call The Question Method® will be contained in the forthcoming book by that title, co-authored with John.

Lastly, I want to again thank my lifelong partner, Jenny Alowa, for always believing in me and encouraging me to "go for it."

1.

Introduction to Second Edition

My purpose in writing both the first and second editions of this work was to fill the void of lack of training for first-time managers and help them gain more satisfaction from that role. Having been thrust into supervision myself without training, I experienced the pains from failure and the self-doubt that was created by my dealing with poor performers. In consulting, I have seen all parties - manager, employee and organization - suffering from this void. My hope is to provide answers to the following:

- What results should I be producing as a manager?

- How do I become more comfortable and confident in delivering those results?

- How do I know if I am doing well?

- How do I know if poor employee performance is due to my lapses or that of the employee?

- How do I become more effective at correcting underperformance and helping employees achieve their full potential?

Two developments have prompted the writing of this new edition.

First, overwhelming research findings year after year show that the traditional supervisory roles and practices are failing both organizations and their employees. "Bad bosses" are the greatest cause of disengagement as well as unwanted turnover and may be the leading contributor to underperformance of organizations.

One takeaway from implementing the 7 Questions method is that lack of fulfillment from work constitutes a spiritual crisis for many in the work force. A second takeaway is that higher performance and happier employees are attainable through a change in management practice. Validation of the methods in the first book prompted a desire to improve clarity and useability in a revised edition.

Secondly, while implementing the 7Q's in organizations has proven the impact of this new approach, it has also uncovered new questions and challenges that need to addressed to help future readers. These are addressed in this edition.

Redefining the supervisor-employee relationship is challenging. It may involve establishing trust where trust has been broken. The 7 Questions work only when and if they reveal new truth. Convincing employees that you want the truth in order for both parties to improve is a precondition for the 7 Questions to add value. A heartfelt communication of why you want to restart will get you there. That new truth can't be "heh, I learned a new tool" or the organization needs to shift to this new method. It needs to be a personal realization, a shift in values, an ability to be vulnerable. More about this in Chapter 4.

Through helping clients implement the 7 Questions, the need for a context for the conversation has become apparent. It cannot be an abstract discussion about employee needs or management missteps. It must be about those needs in light of the current performance on accountabilities and standards.

Clients tell us successful implementation has made their "annual evaluation" process add true value for the first time. Many have replaced the formal evaluation with the 7 Question conversation and action plan.

The 7 Questions method has proven itself capable of shifting organizational culture. Engagement, cooperation, morale, turnover and consequently performance can all be positively impacted. But it requires sustained effort. If it is just another one-shot training program without ongoing support to leaders seeking to make the shift, it will join the history of programs that didn't make a difference. Chapter 8, "Putting the 7 Questions to Work" has been expanded to lay out the lessons learned.

Organizational culture or what is labeled 'level of engagement' is the secret sauce that separates high performing organizations. Your organization may have the same products/services, the same technology, same locations, same pricing, but a competitor with a healthier culture will doom you. Culture dictates the quality of the experience for employees and hence for the customer. Customers can feel a positive culture and value it highly. Culture creates customer loyalty or what Blanchard calls "Raving Fans."[1]

The number one concern of those we have coached is how to handle the "Won't Do" employee. Scores of questions have led to several distinctions on this question that we explore in depth in a new chapter in this edition.

---

1 Blanchard, K. & Bowles, S., Raving Fans , William Morrow, 1993

While adding some new material in this edition, I have also chosen to delete some previous material in order to get to the heart of the matter.

Lastly, several managers with whom we have worked say they have had to read the book several times before trying to put the material to work. To ease this burden, Key Points have been added at the close of each chapter to lessen that burden.

2.

The Role of Manager and Supervisor

Before diving into the 7 Questions and how to use them, let's set the context. How do questions assist managers and supervisors?

The 7 Questions are intended to guide meaningful conversations with direct reports and thus better fulfill the manager/supervisor roles. To fully understand this, let's get clear on these roles and how they add value to an organization.

Manager vs. Supervisor

Overview

The dividing line is thin and is specific to an organization. Generally, supervisors are limited to assuring that what needs to get done is done. The best synonym here would-be overseer. Managers are involved, to varying degrees depending upon their level in the organization, with defining what needs to be done, strategizing on future changes based on shifts in customer needs or market factors, making good use of financial resources and improvement of processes/methods. They are responsible for controlling results and taking corrective actions, some of which may be executed by supervisors.

Supervisors have an entirely internal focus. Managers have both an internal and external focus. The higher up in the organization, the more external the focus. Supervisors are focused on the immediate product or deliverable, the individuals doing the work, and the performance expectations of their assigned team. A typical manager's view broadens to the productivity and profitability of a work center, the efficacy and potential of the individuals within the manager's unit, and the strategic alignment and impact of organization wide decisions.

Usually, supervisors are continuing to do technical work alongside their fellow team members. However, managers should not be doing technical work and in cases where they are required to do so, that technical work should be extremely limited. Managers add value by ensuring a future for the company, reinforcing competitiveness and then assuring that plans/changes are executed well.

Managers often retain the authority to hire, evaluate and terminate employees. Sometimes this gets delegated in whole or in part to supervisors. Again, this role varies by organization.

Supervision can be considered a sub-set of a manager's responsibility. The 7 Questions are applicable in both roles because managers are "overseeing" supervisors. Both play a vital role in development and management of human resources. Human resources are vital to execution, which, at the end of the day, separates market leaders from the also-rans.

Now, let's dive in a bit more deeply.

The Manager Role

I like Lewis A. Allen's[2] definition of management, clear and simple; *"the art and science of helping people use their abilities to the fullest."* It consists of four functions:

Planning: pre-determining a course of action, defining policy and procedure

Organizing: arranging and relating the work to be done so it can be performed effectively by people

Leading: influencing people to take effective action and achieve results

Controlling: assessing and regulating the work in progress to assess the results secured.

Managers assure the future viability of the organization. In addition to being responsible for execution, they are charged with foreseeing and meeting customer needs/wants, strategizing on how to handle competition and defining/driving changes to assure the company's future. At the CEO level, they are largely externally focused. At the lower levels, they are largely internally focused.

If by policy, managers retain authority to hire and terminate, then they are likely completing whatever paperwork the organization may be using for employee evaluation. Supervisors may have input but not the final word. In other organizations, it is the supervisor who is doing the evaluating.

Managers may have responsibility for determining number of positions needed as well as the type, methods and processes used.

---

2 Louis A. Allen, Principles of Professional Management, Louis A. Allen Associates, Inc. (now Louis Allen Worldwide), 1969, 1978 (out of print)

Or, this information may be shared with supervisors. Again, this varies by organization.

The Supervisor Role

Supervision: Def. to be in charge of, ensure that a group of subordinates get out the assigned amount of production, when they are supposed to do it and within acceptable levels of quality, cost and safety

Supervisors assure adherence to accountabilities, priorities, methods and rules. They may or may not be involved in defining them. They instill motivation and ultimately are responsible for the results produced. Synonyms might include overseer or judge. The traditional model is that employees are responsible to the supervisor and the supervisor up the line to a manager for results.

Supervisors determine how best to use the resources provided, how the work group is organized to get the job done, who is assigned to which duties, establishes and enforces deadlines and standards. They may play a role in process improvement.

Supervisors orient new team members, train them as needed, provide clear expectations, offer feedback, deal with performance problems and develop the competencies as well as the confidence of their staff. They should be continuously improving the methods deployed but often they're not given the skills to design and implement new processes with their teams.

The following list details what a supervisor should be providing in service to the organization:

1. On-boarding of well-qualified, motivated team members including understanding of the purpose, vision, values, strategies, priorities and policies of the organization

2. Clarity on the products/services to be produced and the quality standards for each.

3. Training on the methods the team should employ to produce results and the company policies

4. Regular feedback to employees on their performance

5. Delegation of sufficient authority for employees to meet expectations

6. Responsive decisions such that production is not slowed

7. Recognition of accomplishments of team and individuals

8. Definition and execution of development plan for each employee to get them to their full potential

9. Ongoing communications such that employees feel connected to the progress, problems and leadership of the organization

10. An ongoing process to improve the quality, efficiency and effectiveness of methods used.

These ten deliverables are provided both by first-line supervisors and by managers of those supervisors. This list is a tall order to be sure. It often is not fulfilled for the following reasons:

A. Failure to choose as supervisors individuals with a strong interest and aptitude for developing others. There is a myth that someone with strong technical skills will somehow impart these skills to subordinates. But the values and skills needed to transfer technical competence to subordinates differs markedly from development and delivery of your individual technical skills. Being capable of doing does not in turn make an individual capable of training.

Only candidates with an aptitude for developing others should be considered.

B. Supervisors not receiving training on their role. The role of supervisor is often not well defined. Also, new supervisors frequently do not receive training before taking on new responsibilities. The most commonly stated issue by supervisors and managers in our training program is that they were thrust into leadership with little or no guidance or training.

C. Supervisors not being supervised well. You can see the trend here. Once an untrained and underperforming supervisor gets elevated, then the supervisory lapses continue at the next level which leads to more poor supervision throughout the organization.

D. Supervisors have continuing responsibility to produce results themselves leading to insufficient time to develop others. Continuing to do technical work may be a job requirement. Additionally, often supervisors choose to continue technical work because they prefer it or don't trust others to do the work correctly. Hence, the work of developing others doesn't get done and performance of the employee, team and organization suffers. Successful supervisors find satisfaction in seeing others perform well, seeing results over the long haul vs. the immediate gratification of technical work. They have a tolerance for subordinates doing it their way. They have an ability to trust in others even when mistakes, a normal part of the learning process, are occurring. In short, they choose developing others vs. doing the work themselves.

E. Supervisors are unable to make critical values shifts as they transition from doer to overseer.

As explained, supervisors are often promoted because of their work performance and ability to deliver quality products. They are used to being recognized for their individual performance and value being rewarded for work they have done. It is extremely difficult to shift your values to that of someone who feels rewarded when others are recognized for the work they have done. In fact, this is often in direct competition with the values that got you promoted. To help new supervisors make this transition managers need to reward them for the work of their subordinates and recognize them as the source of the good work.

Lack of clarity about these two roles often contributes to underperformance in human resource development.

Are You Adding Value?

W. Edwards Deming, a pioneering theorist and practitioner of continuous quality improvement, defined waste as any effort or expense that does not add value to the product (or service) in the mind of the customer. Supervisors, unless they're doing technical work, are not producing products or services. Instead, they should spend their time developing the staff who do deliver the products and services. The issue is then how to measure whether a supervisor is adding value. Simply examining the list of the ten products they work on isn't enough. Supervisors only add value if, through their efforts, the employees working for them are themselves improving performance. If productivity, product quality or customer experience is not improving, then the supervisors are not adding value.

But organizations tend to treat supervisors as placeholders. That is, if the performance is not declining and turnover is not high, then they are doing their job. No bad news means good news. I disagree and believe that supervisors should be called to and empowered to contribute more value by developing their employees to their full potential.

The Gallup annual engagement survey[3] consistently finds that only 50% of employees know what is expected of them. Only 19% agree they receive routine feedback. Only 17% report meaningful feedback that helps them to "learn, grow and do their jobs better." Only 14% report that performance reviews "inspire them to improve." The data supports a finding that the majority of supervisors are not adding value through their management work.

Why is this happening? Let's explore how difficult it is to add value through your employees.

Again, Gallup survey data[4] consistently finds that 35% of employees are engaged and highly motivated, 13% are disengaged and the balance have variable motivation, i.e., they have good days and bad days. Those with variable motivation are influenceable by good supervision that understands and addresses the source of the variation. Those with low motivation are indeed challenging and need active management. Some employees may improve but others should be encouraged to consider other employment options or terminated.

If your organization fits these parameters, 35% of people who work for you will likely need only encouragement and opportunity

3 Gallup, "What 'Meaningful Feedback' Means to Millennials", Adam Hickman, Workplace, January 29, 2020
4 Gallup, "Four Factors Driving Record-High Employee Engagement Scores", Jim Harter, Workplace, February 4, 2020

to find their way to higher performance. More than 50% will need ongoing monitoring and feedback followed by partnering on a game plan in order to achieve consistent and improved performance. That's not easy. The final 13% are indeed challenging. They may show up as motivated, have lots of "reasons" for their lapses in performance and will avoid conversations to address them.

The balance of this book addresses how to determine which of these groupings your employees are in, how to evaluate your own efforts to meet their needs and how to develop a plan that has both you and your employees adding value.

Terms Going Forward

For the rest of the book, I will only use the term manager. Here are my reasons:

- The role of "overseer" assumes that without someone looking over the employee's shoulder, the work won't get done or won't get done right. But the research points to the majority of employees being self-motivated. Being an overseer becomes demeaning and doesn't add value.

- Supervisor feeds into the narrative of "bad bosses" which is the number one reason for unwanted employee turnover.

- The term supervisor falls short of identifying a person responsible for ensuring that employees reach their potential.

- Supervisor lets the organization off the hook from a) recruiting those with aptitude for people development rather than just technical skills and b) providing the training needed to really develop employees.

Consequently, my approach is that there are multiple levels of management in an organization. Front-line managers may continue to do technical work but they add value by developing others, not just looking over their shoulder.

Evaluate Yourself

Have you had that "aha" moment yet? Do you feel that you don't have time for the onboarding, training, coaching and mentoring? Remember <u>you only add value to the organization as a front-line manager if you improve the performance of direct reports.</u> If you are not spending time striving to move your employees toward their potential, then you need to address why that is so. The following discussion will give you tools that will help but only if you commit yourself to the role as defined above.

Front-line managers don't often think in these terms. There is a subtle, but important difference between, "How can I do more to get more?" vs. "How can I get more?" The former statement reflects an understanding of responsibility to develop others. The latter reflects more of a crack the whip mentality. The 7 Questions are intended to help you understand how to develop others. The Questions are designed to make it easier to establish honesty, openness and to build the relationship needed for both manager and direct report to learn and grow. Remember, this applies to leaders/managers at all levels.

The Role of Manager and Supervisor — Key Points

1. Manager and supervisor share in common a responsibility to assure good results from employees. For supervisors, this is their primary responsibility. In varying degrees by level in the organization managers focus on assuring the future viability of the organization, plan and execute changes and

have their attention outside the company on customer and competitor. Supervisors focus on their teams. Supervisor is a subset of a manager's responsibilities.

2. Supervisor, traditionally defined as overseer, is usually not responsible for, trained or empowered to develop employee potential. Today's employees are largely self-motivated, making overseer an antiquated concept that does not add value to the organization.

3. The limited role of supervisor is antiquated and does not add value. A more robust role as "coach" or manager who is responsible for getting employees to their potential is the way forward.

4. These roles are specific to organizations and defined by accountabilities and authorities.

5. To be effective in developing people, one needs a shift in values from technical work, motivation, aptitude in human relations skills and training.

6. Most organizations underperform because supervision is not focused on and invested in as well as because untrained supervisors tend to choose to do technical work rather than develop people.

7. Adding value means improving the performance of those who work with you.

8. The antiquated classification of supervisor should be replaced by front-line manager or coach.

3.

The Two Types of Performance Problems

Ken Blanchard has said, there are two categories of people problems, those that are "Can't Do" and those that are "Won't Do."

"Can't Do" problems stem from lack of aptitude, training, skill or confidence. They arise from inaction or ineffective action by the manager. Ineffective action could include selecting the wrong candidate, e.g., one without aptitude or motivation to learn and perform. Inaction might be lack of orientation/onboarding, unclear direction, lack of coaching to reinforce confidence or build skills. But for the lack of appropriate training and assistance from the manager, the employee could do the work. Hence, it is the manager who is responsible for solving this type of problem.

"Won't Do" problems stem from lack of motivation and conscious or unconscious unwillingness to deliver the results required of them. Motivation may decline because of any number of individual issues and concerns; personal problems, grievances with the organization or manager, lack of inspiration for the work or product, etc. Some situations can be alleviated by the manager but ultimately, they must be resolved by the employee.

The challenge for managers is to determine which type of problem exists and then take effective action to solve it. Without clarity on which problem exists, an effective plan of correction cannot be developed or carried out.

The 7 Questions are intended to help you make the call: "Am I, as manager, responsible for this problem (Can't Do)?" or "Should I be holding the employee responsible for the problem (Won't Do)?" Without certainty about the type of problem, managers are frozen in inaction wondering "is it me?" or "is it him/her?" Meanwhile the performance problems continue.

Later chapters will address handling the two types of problem in detail. For now, here is a brief explanation of each type as well as issues that overlap both types.

1. Can't Do Problems

"Can't Do" problems arise because the employee has not been given the tools for success. "Can't Do" problems are typically caused by one or more of the following::

- Lack of pre-requisite skills and experience. A faulty hiring process can result in an employee having no chance of success. While it is true that on the job training can be effective, unless an employee has the basic skills and experience needed for the position, the individual will feel as if he or she will be set up for failure. Especially in managerial positions, it is challenging to recover from a poor start in which employees feel as if they have to train their manager.

- Lack of clarity on responsibilities. Lack of or conflicting direction as to products, priorities or deadlines. The lack of clarity can arise because of 1) organization structure issue with multiple sources of supervision or responsibilities being shared by more than one position, or 2) inconsistent messages from a supervisor. In short, the employees can't do it because they don't know what it is.

- Lack of understanding of the manager's standard for a good work product. The employees may have the skills and experience required for a given responsibility but they don't know your standard for that responsibility or work product. Thus, again, they can't do it because you have not informed them about your "expectations."

- Lack of or unclear rules and procedures. These include pre-scribed methods, delegated authorities and more informal rules. Each organization has its own culture. The culture can be thought of as a set of norms of behavior. Sometimes these are unwritten or not communicated and the new employee can stick out like a sore thumb, e.g., wear the wrong clothes, engage in type of humor or other behavior that is frowned upon, not respect the time of others or fail to meet the norms of teams. Being out of alignment with norms impacts the performance of teams. Again, the employees can't fit in with the culture or the company's way of doing business if they don't know what your way is.

- Lack of feedback. The first time employees take a shot at doing what they understand is expected, they need feedback on whether they did or did not get it right. Without feedback, they may needlessly modify their method the next time out. The uncertainty arising from lack of feedback can lead to reduced productivity as well as inconsistent quality of work product.

- Lack of cooperation/support from team members or other teams.

- Insufficient resources or authority/timely decisions to meet expectations

"Can't Do" problems arise most often for new employees but can also occur any time accountabilities or expectations change. Each time you assign an employee a new responsibility or task, you need to make clear your standards for the work product. In short, you have to get "Yes" answers anew to the 7 Questions.

2. Confidence Problems

Overlaying Can't Do and Won't Do problems is the employee's inability to operate independently or initiate change or take risks. This is attributed primarily to lack of confidence and/or fear of failure. This can arise from the employee's read of the manager, e.g., making a mistake will bring on the manager's wrath. Or it could be sourced in the employee's history with other managers or the employee's mental state at any given time. Those who lack confidence struggle to finish projects because they fear their work is never good enough. Hence, there may be lots of activity but no real product emerges.

In other cases, managers continue to hold employees accountable but literally don't let them do the work on their own. The employee may not lack confidence but the manager lacks confidence in the employee. The manager complains that the employee is not getting things done and consequently, the manager has to do the employee's work. This creates a vicious cycle because the manager has not developed a pathway to gain confidence in delegating work to employees.

If fear of repercussions or a sense that the manager lacks confidence in the employee, then the manager can correct the problem. If perfectionism leading to inability to complete is the source, the employee must correct the problem but the manager can have influence here.

3. The Baggage You Inherit

You inherit the impact of whatever experience your employees have had with former bosses or other authority figures. The experience will color how they view and respond to you. That experience may prove to be a barrier to getting truthful answers to the 7 Questions and to partnering for better performance.

As an example, at a welcoming party for a new office manager I once hired, I became curious about why the new employee was so distant. We made a great connection during the hiring process but at the party he avoided me like the plague, moving away from me whenever I approached. When I inquired about his change in behavior, he responded with, "You are now my boss." I replied, "Yes, that is the hat that I wear, but we are in a social setting so why would you avoid me?" He replied, "You now have control over my life." I learned that he had been the victim of punishing, arbitrary supervision in the past and was anxious about starting work with an unknown boss. We worked our relationship out quickly, but had we not, he would have avoided taking initiative or making decisions and he would have fallen well short of his enormous potential.

In this example, there was a shared responsibility. The employee brought in baggage that could have negatively impacted his performance or the speed of his development. In a sense, it was his responsibility to make his history known and ultimately controlled whether he would come to trust me. My responsibility was to spot this potential problem and take the necessary steps to prevent it from hindering the employee's performance and potential.

4. Your Impact

When there is turnover in a position, research shows it takes from six to nine months to regain the level of performance in that position. The critical variable here is how well the manager does in filling the gaps, i.e., eliminating the Can't Do problems. Most employee orientation programs are deficient and many managers complain that they simply don't have enough time to execute employee development because they have more pressing problems or demands to continue to produce technical work.

Filling the gaps in training, direction and coaching, followed by feedback and rewards for performance solve Can't Do problems. The 7 Questions will help you diagnose which element is deficient and then dialogue about the specific actions both parties can take to fill the gaps. Using these questions should enable you to shorten the time required to get a new employee up to speed.

5. Won't Do Problems

Won't Do problems arise because the employee consciously or sub-consciously is choosing not to perform as directed. That is, if you have delivered the products of supervisors/managers as verified by an honest "yes" answer to the 7 Questions, then poor performance is an employee choice on some level.

The challenge is that employees with such problems will mask them. They always appear to be busy, engaged, committed, and hard-working. But, at the end of the day, they aren't producing a product or not the one that you want. Instead, they are producing confusion. Generally, you don't press them because, outwardly, they seem to be your best employees. When you do press, they state that they didn't understand or were confused about the work but will not provide specifics so that you can fill in the gaps. Furthermore, they sow confusion among co-workers. Teams with such members are frequently in disarray and have high rates of sick days.

When pressed, using the 7 Questions and other questions, Won't Do employees will speak in generalities about problems or barriers to their producing what you want. They may say that "everyone is confused." The end result here is that you won't have the information needed to solve the problem because the problem can never get defined.

So, the only way to really diagnose a Won't Do problem is by a) looking at statistics that bear out a lack of production and b) employing the 7 Questions but finding that in the end you have nothing tangible to correct. That is, you have qualified "yes" answers to all the questions. So, you are left with a mystery. Well, there is no mystery here. It's a Won't Do problem.

Won't Do problems arise for a number of reasons including:

1. the employee has lost motivation (or never had it)
2. the employee is seeking revenge or to even the score for some perceived injustice (e.g., passed over for promotion)
3. the employee no longer supports the mission
4. the employee is experiencing a personal problem (e.g., divorce, addiction)
5. the employee has grievances with co-workers

6. the employee has a history of failure prompting a strategy to mask non-performance rather than risk future failures

Ultimately, the employee owns such problems. The circumstances may be understandable, even tragic, but this should not justify your taking ownership. You can't fix the problem but you can support the employee who is solving the problem.

Won't Do problems may justify lenience in approving leave or time off for counseling, even investing in some form of help; but they do not justify continuing to tolerate unsatisfactory performance. Whatever supportive steps you choose, they must be coupled with a tightened accountability for results. Ultimately, the road to recovery for a damaged soul is productivity. It is the basis for all positive morale.

The hurdle that well-meaning managers need to overcome is putting the welfare of the team and organization first.

Furthermore, not handling employees with Won't Do problems erodes the standing of you as the leader. It represents a failure to provide both order and safety in the form of fairness. An employee not meeting standards leads to other employees enduring some measure of chaos and picking up added work for which they are usually not recognized or rewarded.

Truthful answers to the 7 Questions will provide clarity about whether you have done all you can and whether the employee owns the problem you both face. Having the employee agree that you have done all that you can should strengthen your resolve to confront the employee's choice to not perform. Chapter 9 is devoted to how to handle Won't Do problems once they are properly diagnosed.

The Two Types of Performance Problems — Key Points

1. The two types of problems are *Can't Do* and *Won't Do*. *Can't Do's* are correctable by and the responsibility of the manager. *Won't Do's* are a conscious or unconscious choice of employee not to produce what is needed and are correctable only if the employee chooses to change behavior.

2. Managers can get frozen in inaction trying to decipher who is to blame for non-performance. The 7 Questions are designed to bring clarity to this question.

3. *Can't Do* problems include not knowing the manager's standards for work products and can arise any time that new responsibilities are assigned.

4. *Can't Do* problems can also arise when there is a lack of support, resources or timely decisions needed to meet expectations.

5. Lack of confidence by employees can lead to inability and/or unwillingness to act independently or produce final products to be evaluated. Managers can effectively build confidence in employees but they need to be aware of employees' background, such as whether the employees had a history of abuse by authority figures.

6. *Won't Do* problems are challenging to diagnose because the employees often attempt to mask the truth, sow confusion, and derail problem solving. In the end, you must make a judgement that you have done all you can to get a "yes" response to the 7 Questions and recognize that the employee is choosing to continue to not produce what is needed. Don't let an extended problem solving conversation on the 7Questions or seeming busyness by the employee

confuse you. Simply look at the statistics to determine if finished products are being produced, whether those products meet standards and whether the level of production meets that of co-workers.

4.

Why A Change in Role and Approach Matters

The biggest hurdle in transitioning from supervisor to coach and from judge to performance partner is communicating to employees that this shift is sincere. In short, you have to come up with your own "Big Why" to explain that you're now seeking to evaluate yourself and define how you can add more value.

Depending on the prior experience of the employee with you, this new approach may trigger a cynical or guarded response. You have to be genuine and believable to overcome resistance. You must craft a personal story to explain this change in your work tactics. Simply saying "I read this book" or "I went to this training and want to try this out" will not prompt truthful responses when you ask people where you have fallen short. Responding would be too big a risk for many employees.

I offer the following story in the hope that it can influence your role and responsibility with regard to the welfare of those who work for you. The experience was enough to convince me to not take what I see and hear at face value but to investigate further to uncover the truth about why an employee is not performing and whether the person is willing to change course.

Gena

On my first day as Deputy Commissioner of Department of Health for the Commonwealth of Massachusetts, I was given a general orientation, told which functions within the Department were my responsibility and then shown to my office. On the way down the hall from the Commissioner's office, the Director of Administration offered some advice. "You will be sharing two secretaries with two other Deputy Commissioners. One secretary is Gena. She has been here for twenty-six years and hasn't worked a lick in the last twenty or so. My advice is that you simply ignore that she exists because you won't get any work out of her and you can't fire her."

As I entered the suite of offices, I spotted Gena at a desk immediately to the left. I recognized her without introduction because she looked totally miserable. Her complexion was gray in color, her eyes sunken with deep circles beneath them and she had a sour look on her face. Her desk showed no signs of activity and her typewriter (yes, it was that long ago) still had its cover on at mid-morning.

I said, "Hello." She did not respond and I moved on for introductions to the others. The phone rang shortly thereafter, and Gena ignored it.

I didn't think much of the incident at first. But after days of walking by Gena and seeing no signs of productivity, life, communication, humor or enjoyment, it began to wear on me. Also, it became apparent that I was going to be buried with work and would need real assistance.

So, after about a week, I asked Gena to come into my office and chat. I think she was startled by the request. I began as follows, "Gena, what they told me about you is that you have been here twenty-six years, that you haven't done any real work for the last twenty, and that I should not expect that to change or to try and make it so. Well, I'm just not comfortable assuming that based on what other people tell me, so I would like to hear from you about that."

Gena's eyes came alive and were riveted on me and I saw something that I had not seen since I got there. Gena began talking, and almost immediately the tears began to flow. "When I started here, I worked hard and no one seemed to notice or care. So, after several years I decided to stop working and see what happened. Well, nothing happened. They didn't seem to care about that either, so I just stopped working and that's where I have been ever since." I was stunned. I responded with, "Well, Gena, I do care. I don't want you sitting here being miserable and not feeling productive. Besides, I have lots of work to do and could really use the help."

Gena's backbone stiffened and her face came alive. She said, "Well, then, let's get to work." She marched out of my office, went to her desk and uncovered her typewriter, then came back in with a steno pad (again a testament to my age) to ask me what I needed done. As she came to my office, she entreated the other support staff to get to work.

Thereafter, not only did Gena achieve high productivity, but her entire physical appearance and demeanor in the office changed. The scowl was gone. She was gruff by nature, but her humor came out and she genuinely enjoyed herself. She would regularly growl at those who weren't productive. She became my protector. Better yet, she made me fresh baklava (Gena was Greek) every week.

Those who had been with the Department for years noticed the change and asked me half-jokingly, "What drugs are you giving her?" All I was giving her was the opportunity to contribute and an appreciation for her contributions. It was simple and miraculous.

The single question I asked Gena won't resolve most situations and employees rarely make the sudden or dramatic shift that Gena made on her own. But this story demonstrates the power of honest conversation, of learning the true reason behind an employee's demeanor and attitude, and gaining mutual understanding. The 7 Questions can reveal the root of the performance problem and the needed elements of action for each party to solve it.

It takes courage to ask these questions of an unhappy employee. Good leaders feel responsible for the condition of their employees. But, if they're anxious, they will fear that the fault lies with their own action or inaction and in fact, may avoid asking why. I wasn't anxious because I had inherited Gena's condition. Whatever happened to Gena could not be my fault. It was easy to ask. But, having asked and gotten such a positive result, I permanently overcame any reserve that I had to find the truth with future employees. What I have seen time and again is that leaders who have the courage to ask find that the truth is better than any explanation they feared. I encourage you to seek the truth. It is the only means to better performance, regardless the response.

To this day, I remain grateful to Gena for this powerful lesson. My relationships with employees changed forever. My hope is that this story has brought to mind a similar experience or has kindled your interest in discovering what is really going on with your colleagues and employees. The chapters that follow are intended to arm you with tools to discover that truth.

You and your employees spend the majority of your waking hours together. Everyone deserves an experience that is genuine, productive and rewarding. Work should be what energizes us. We should not have to burden family with propping us back up day after day to return to work that robs us of energy and joy.

To make the shift to performance coach and to an honest relationship with those with whom you work, you will need to discover and communicate your own truth about why making this shift is important to you. While you may fear hearing the truth, your employees are likely to have greater fear in sharing with you. You need to set a foundation of trust upon which to build the road to better performance. But, before moving on to learn how to accomplish this, ask yourself whether what you have read to this point rings true for you. Is there a story akin to Gena's story that you can relate from your own experience that will motivate you to make the shift and make your first conversation genuine and trustworthy?

Why This Matters — Key Points

1. Uncovering the truth about why an employee is not performing can release untapped motivation and performance. The truth is the entry point to a relationship resulting in partnership to reach full potential.

2. This one-on-one conversation must begin with relaying your own truth about why you are shifting how you manage and that you want to learn how you can add value to develop employee potential. You have to establish trust to gain the truth.

3. You must overcome the fear of hearing about your shortcomings by understanding that it is the only road to both parties prospering.

5.

The 7 Questions

Overview

A conversation with a direct report about performance often raises anxiety for both parties and may be avoided for that reason.

For the employee, the discomfort likely stems from experience with past annual evaluations. These reviews may have focused on "What I didn't do right" rather than "what went well." Or, the employee is not feeling positive about performance at this point and doesn't really wish to talk about it.

For the manager, some of the rationalizations used to avoid these conversations include:

- *Who am I to judge? I don't feel that great about my own performance, or I don't have an objective basis for my judgment.*

- *I don't want to hurt or dampen motivation.*

- *We have an open and relaxed culture and don't really need to have regular "performance" conversations.*

- *What will be the criticism regarding me?*

- *I know I see the situation differently than the employee. We have discussed before to no avail and there is no point in revisiting.*

- *I don't believe in the evaluation process we are using.*

But, without honest dialogue, employee development or performance improvement won't occur, and the manager will not be adding value to the organization.

The 7 Questions are designed to ease these conversations and make them liberating and possibly even uplifting to both parties. In any relationship when the air is cleared and both sides have been honest, there is a sense of a new beginning and new possibilities. Employing the 7 Questions as scripted will focus the conversation and pave the way for improvement by both parties.

You may decide to share the script with the employee before having the conversation or you may just introduce the questions yourself, possibly go thru them more than once to get complete answers.

Here is a suggested dialogue for opening these conversations in a non-threatening way.

Set the Context

Whether or not you share the Questions before the conversation, you will need to define and present your personal reasons for using a different approach. Then:

Extend an invitation for a meeting by stating something like, "I'd like to sit down and revisit what we are doing to optimize your success here. I have a new approach that makes it easy for us to engage in discussion and learn how we might better work together to get the results we both want."

At the meeting, begin with, "I view the manager-employee relationship as a partnership. We both have responsibility to make the most of it. I want to learn how I can better fulfill my responsibility as a partner. Then, I want to prepare and plan for both of us to take action on what we discover. Do you have any questions or thoughts before we start?"

"All right. What I am going to do is ask you a series of 7 Questions. Each question requires only a 'yes' or 'no' answer. Each question focuses on whether I have fulfilled one of my responsibilities to you in setting you up for success. If there is more that I can do in any of the areas covered by the question, then I want you to answer with 'no' or 'somewhat.' If you do, then I am going to ask you what is missing, inconsistent or unclear that would be of benefit to you. At the end we will develop a plan of action for both of us and set a time to review our progress."

"Before asking the Questions, I am going to give you my take on how you are performing on each of your responsibilities including how well you work with others and adhere to the core values and policies of the organization. For each responsibility, I will note whether you are performing at or above standards, below standards or produce inconsistent performance etc. I am then going to ask the Questions to determine how best I can assist in boosting your performance in the areas noted.

"For each Question, if the answer is 'yes,' but you have answered the question yourself rather than getting what is needed from me, then I want you to answer 'no.' For example, if I ask whether you are clear on what is expected of you, you may have

figured it out yourself. But you are not clear on whether my expecta-
tions are the same as yours or maybe whether the priorities re. those
expectations are the same. So, if you don't have certainty about my
expectations of you, then the answer should be 'no.' Make sense?"

Another point is that if you answer "yes" to all the questions,
it leaves me with no way to add value to you or the organization in
your current role. My goal in this first meeting is to get a "no" on
one or more one or more of the 7 Questions so that I can add value.

If your answers are "yes" to the Questions about your current
responsibilities and you are performing at or above standards, then
we should explore your personal goals for learning and advance-
ment, then work on a game plan for those.

"When we get to the end, we will agree on a course of action
based on your answers. Any questions? Ready to begin?"

The 7 Questions

Then, go through each of the questions. They are as follows:

1. *Do you know what is expected of you?*

2. *Do you know what good performance looks like in your job as defined by your supervisor?*

3. *Do you get feedback on the results that you produce?*

4. *Do you have sufficient authority to carry out your responsibilities?*

5. *Do you get timely decisions in the areas where you don't have authority?*

6. *Do you have the data, resources and support needed to meet what is expected of you?*

7. *Do you get credit for the good results that you produce?*

Getting to "No"

Avoid the tendency to receive a "yes" response and feel good about it. After all, the Questions represent a sort of report card on how you are doing. But these initial "yes" responses may not be honest. Those we have coached tell us that in some cases one needs to go thru the Questions several times or even set up a follow-up meeting in order to get to an honest "no," "generally" or "sometimes." It may be that your message to set the context wasn't yet believable or that you have an employee with substantial fear coming from experience with past managers..

The other possibility is that you receive "yes" answers but the performance is not up to standard. The employee is hoping that the "yes's" will end the conversation as they don't want being a Won't Do to be found out. If that is the case, the next question might be, "Well then how do you explain not performing well in........................"?

The balance of the book discusses use of the 7 Questions in detail, gives suggestions on follow-up questions to get clarity and explores how to develop a joint action plan.

Question #1 – Expectations

David

Early in my career, I established and managed a health project funded through President Lyndon Johnson's War on Poverty. The project entailed organizing Alaska Native leaders from fifteen villages spread over 44,000 square miles. The intent was to empower them to provide for their own healthcare and to demonstrate to the Indian Health Service (the Federal agency charged with fulfilling the treaty obligation to provide health services to Native Americans) a new model of primary care that would deliver better health outcomes.

The project was successful from its inception. About seven years into it, the board of directors issued a strong directive wanting more progress in bringing Alaska Native people into high-level management positions. My initial strategy was to create a new position of Director of Ambulatory Services. I then went searching for a candidate with management potential.

I found David in California. Born and raised in Alaska, he had worked his way up to a supervisory position in a hospital laboratory. His technical training was as a lab technician. He had virtually no managerial or supervision training. I was counting on his technical experience, intelligence, ambition and goodwill from the clinic nursing staff as well as my support to propel him to greatness.

David moved north. I gave him a job description, two-days of orientation (health system overview, policies, facility tour, etc.) and lots of words of encouragement. Within two weeks, he was in my office with serious doubts about his ability to succeed and those nurses would visit complaining that not only was he not adding value, he was making matters worse.

I counseled David to sit down with the nurses and really listen to their concerns, use his common sense to define solutions and to work with his staff to refine solutions to their problems. Well, that didn't work. He continued to frequent my office asking for help. The nurses continued to complain and the morale of everyone declined.

The effect of my counsel of David was to send him back to the lion's den with a false sense of confidence (actually I don't believe I accomplished that). David's strategy to overcome being uncertain was to act overly confident and play his authority card. He didn't want to ask his staff for help or to collaborate for solutions because he was uncomfortable facing them. Feeling like an imposter, David tried to soldier on by pretending.

The cycle of David meeting with me, followed by my meeting with the nurses to plead for their patience, was repeated over and over for the next six months. At that point, David resigned and returned to California. I never heard from him again, but I fear to this day that I permanently destroyed his self-confidence and stunted his career. What had been a real opportunity to develop an effective leader was missed because of my own lapses. It's a lesson that haunts me to this day.

In retrospect, David was the wrong hire to step into such a high-pressure position without mentoring. He should not have been put into the ring. The elevation to being responsible for a very busy clinic with a staff of stressed-out, highly trained professionals was too steep a gradient. I naively assumed that David's earnest ambition, his innate intelligence, common sense and my words of encouragement would be all it would take.

At the time, I was disappointed that the clinic staff was not more patient and supportive of my strategy. Looking back, I see that they were rightly focused on delivering the best care and trying to meet the high demand for services. Inserting David into the mix only added uncertainty, more problems and delay. It was not supportive of them either.

I erred in not anticipating or forewarning David of the challenge. I never made clear what he was expected to deliver. His job descriptions, like most, certainty didn't inform him. Going into a new job armed with only the job description is a recipe for failure.

So, what did David need to know? First, I should have defined more clearly his accountabilities and my expectations. He needed a complete picture of what a well-run clinic should look like and what it should produce. Spending some time interning, observing a well-run clinic and its leader might have done the trick.

Next, I should have explained to him how I would assess that the clinic was well run, what good performance looks like from my perspective. I think all that David understood was that if the nurses weren't complaining, all was well.

The challenge David faced was that the majority of his staff had more training and experience than he did. The road to success for him would have been to become a good facilitator at team meetings in which staff would collaborate on solutions; to use their skills rather than be threatened by them. That way, he could have become proficient while not doing damage to the operation. But that takes a strong individual, i.e., one who is willing to be somewhat vulnerable. I never laid that out as an expectation or strategy for success. Nor did I model being a good facilitator of solutions, co-facilitate with him or coach him. Consequently, David did not know what was expected, so he just behaved like a boss as he pictured one and hoped that would work.

Reflecting back, my failure to deliver clear direction was based on a wrong-headed belief that telling him what to do was an insult and would do damage. I was essentially delegating to the clinic nursing staff the training of David to be effective. David's failure was to adopt an authoritarian leader role which I never spotted nor did I tell him that role wasn't what I intended..

An Example from the Other End of the Spectrum

David knew relatively nothing about the expectations I had of him. The lapse was no expectations.

Later in my career, I experienced an organization where the opposite was in play. I was engaged by a large health insurance company in the Pacific Northwest via a relatively new vice-president in charge of a major division. He sought planning help to clarify direction for his team. Although he was responsible for his team, management above him was undermining him by mandating goals. The result was confusion amongst the group about priorities.

During my initial meeting with the group, I asked them, "What's expected of you now? What are the priorities and how do you know?" The answer was that an astounding 125 goals had been assigned to them. I then asked the group, "Well, when you come to work, how do you decide what to go to work on?" They responded, "Well, we just wait to hear about the goal for the day because at some point in the hallway or at the coffee pot, an existing or new goal will be presented as an emergency."

In short, there were so many goals that goals had become meaningless. The overwhelm was debilitating. In the end, the effect was no clear direction.

Why This Matters

Both David and the insurance team were unclear as what to produce, what the priorities were or how they were going to be evaluated. Lack of clear expectations causes uncertainty, caution and low performance. A small percentage of employees will figure it out for themselves, but this can be perilous. They know you will be judging their performance at some point and they want to know how you are keeping score. What results are most important to you? At best, in the absence of certainty, there will be caution in taking action. You will be asked countless questions because employees fear making a mistake. At worst, there will either be no action or actions that don't add value or potentially do harm. That's why communicating clear expectations matters.

How to Get to "Yes" on Question 1?

Give the employee a clear and thorough description of why the position exists, what it is expected to produce (not activity but completed products/services) and how success in the position will be measured. When asking the question, be sure that you are asking whether you have made clear your personal expectations rather than the employee figuring it out on his own or from others as that puts misunderstanding at risk.

Most job descriptions don't deliver this information. Job descriptions are largely used to compare the value of the various jobs in your organization for purposes of placing them on the salary scale. They have little utility as a tool in managing.

An example of a job description that would have been helpful to both David and I might look like the following:

Clinic Manager

Purpose:

To assure a smoothly functioning and high-quality outpatient services operation through effective supervision, process design and problem solving.

Products of Position:

- Measures of and standards for clinic performance defined and maintained.

- Clinic measures monitored and problems, i.e., below standard performance, identified.

- Solutions to performance problems defined and implemented with clinic staff.

- Regular meetings held with staff to gain input about problems and ideas for improved performance.

- Processes involving diagnostic (e.g., lab, x-ray) and support services monitored and problems identified.

- Meetings conducted with diagnostic and support services to identify and resolve problems, improve performance.

- Staff members evaluated semi-annually and plans for improvement developed.

- Patient feedback gathered, assessed and utilized to improve service

Measures of Success:

- Number of patient complaints or results of patient satisfaction surveys

- Employee turnover

- Number of patients seen per provider per hour

- Audit results on conformance with treatment protocols

Had I provided all of this, one of the two alternatives to the unhappy outcome with David may have resulted: 1) he may not have taken the job knowing what was expected, or 2) he and I would have had a much more productive dialogue about his training or coaching needs. With training or effective coaching, he might have succeeded.

If I had asked the question, "Do you know or have I made clear what is expected of you?" David's honest answer would have either been "no" or "do a good job." I would have discovered that I was at fault.

During the first thirty to ninety days on the job or on when a new assignment within an existing job has occurred, check back on whether the answer to the question is still "yes." After some time on the job, the employee may have clarifying questions or their own ideas about the expectations, both of which would be important to discuss. Or, like the insurance group that was overwhelmed by 125 goals, you may have sent signals about expectations or priorities that are very different from the expectations you laid out at the beginning. In short, dialogue on clarity of expectations is not a one and done exercise but an ongoing need as organizations are constantly changing.

Should you get a "no" response, here are some additional areas you may wish to probe in your dialogue in order to come up with an action plan to get to "yes":

- *Did the strategic plan or other direction bring up any questions for you regarding what is expected or what the priorities might be?*

- *Has any confusion been created about what is expected of you either through my actions or decisions of the management team?*

- *Is there any confusion about authorities that impact the clarity of expectations? For example, are others on your team seeing expectations and priorities differently?*

- *Are expectations of other departments or managers creating conflicts in the expectations or priorities of your department?*

- *Are there instances where shared responsibility is creating uncertainty?*

- *Are there any policies that are creating uncertainty about expectations?*

- *Are the expectations realistic?*

- *Do you feel confident about being able to meet those expectations?*

- *Are there skills sets or experience you feel you need to improve to deliver on those expectations?*

- *Are there expectations that you don't feel are needed or that you aren't motivated to deliver?*

Question #2 – Good Performance

JoAnn

I hired JoAnn as an Office Manager/Consultant shortly after she arrived in state. She was highly educated, extremely smart and brought several years of experience from a Chicago-based consulting firm. I considered myself lucky to have her. I thought she wouldn't need much training. I could just keep focused on efforts to grow my consulting business, and she would cover my back on all things admin.

A few months into her tenure, I overheard her handling of a client phone call. She was abrupt and communicated disinterest. I had negative visions of what that client must be thinking about her and my business.

When JoAnn finished the call, I remarked that I wasn't happy with how she handled it. In disbelief, she asked why. I responded with, "Well, what I want clients or prospects to experience when they talk with us is a sincere interest in them and why they are calling. I want them to get our willingness to take as long as necessary to understand why they called and to get them what they need. Instead, what I thought that client experienced was 'we aren't interested in you or your problem.' And, that is not satisfactory."

JoAnn was miffed and came back with, "Well, I didn't know that. Furthermore, my boss in Chicago considered time on the phone to be wasted because it wasn't billable. He was constantly harping on me to get off the phone."

It took a while for us to work this out. Why? JoAnn rightly objected that my standard had not been made known to her when she started. She felt that she had been set up to make a mistake, to disappoint me and to be made wrong. This could have been prevented. She was right.

By the way, this employment arrangement didn't last long. We didn't get off on a good footing and we never quite recovered from it.

Lesson learned? Don't assume that because someone has performed a given duty for someone else that person will do the job the way you want it done. What usually doesn't get revealed until violated are your hidden standards, the pet peeves or critical distinctions that separate a great product/service from one that is just okay.

Why this Matters

When it comes time to talk about or evaluate performance, if the manager employs a set of standards that have not been shared, this can easily create a conflict. Instead of intentionally setting up the employee to succeed, the manager unintentionally sets the employee up to lose on some level because he or she didn't know the goal or standard. This violates the concept of fairness discussed previously. Providing clarity on standards at the very beginning of the manager - employee relationship gives the employee the greatest chance of meeting those standards and winning early on.

How to Get to "Yes"

1. Understand that you have your own standards regarding how the responsibilities you assign should be performed. Those standards may be hidden or you may not be able to articulate them, but they are there. Be specific and communicate the small things that are pet peeves for you. An employee will sense that you are not thrilled with the results but he won't know why you're unhappy unless you communicate. With each new hire or each new responsibility assigned, take the time to get a clear picture in your own mind as to what an ideal handling of that responsibility would look like. Then, share it.

2. Encourage dialogue as the employee may have a viewpoint that leads to good outcomes for customers that may not be familiar to you. If so, be open to amending your own standards.

3. To help define your standards, look back on those who have previously been in the position, describe the performance

of a peak performer and then define the performance of someone whose performance didn't meet your standards. Being clear on these two points will enable you to give clarity to the new employee about what will be key when you are evaluating their performance. What matters to you? Is it timeliness? Being error free? Grammar? Is it attitude? Being a self-starter? How about productivity? Being a team player?

4. Understand and communicate what is important to you. In the example of JoAnn, it was not that she failed to answer the calls, it was how she handled them and how her attitude made them feel.

The dialogue might include comments like these:

- *"What's particularly important to me is that ...."*
- *"Basic standards are to achieve.................."*
- *"Achieving ....would be a real bonus."*
- *"The errors or omissions that particularly concern me are........................"*
- *"What I have found with others is that .... is particularly challenging"*
- *"I have noticed in the past that.................. This is the area in which I think we don't have the same picture about what is important."*

5. Deliver or communicate your expectations up front. Often, managers don't do this because they think it will be perceived as an insult to the employee's intelligence. Or, that the employee will learn this on their own over time. Of course, at some point, you have to let go and let employees

try but empower them to get it right by making expectations and standards clear.

To get over being squeamish about this discussion, explain that you aren't going through your standards because you think the employee does not know what to do, but because you want to clarify what's important to you so there are no hidden standards. Consider sharing that not doing this in the past has been a problem for others.

Question #3 – Feedback

Evelyn

Evelyn had been my executive secretary for years. I couldn't have asked for a more loyal and committed source of support. I could depend on her for any task at any moment. In truth, I was spoiled rotten.

Over time as I saw her commitment to our success grow, I began to see some troubling signs. What I observed was her asserting authority she did not have over other clerical staff in the executive suite.

The secretary to the CEO possesses considerable informal power. That person sees and hears virtually every communication. That position is essentially the nerve center for the organization. The executive secretary becomes a confidant, e.g., the first person the CEO looks to for venting frustration. They often know the boss better than anyone in the organization. The other employees' respond to what that person says and does as a way of gauging where the boss might be coming from on any given day.

Evelyn was using that informal power to get what she wanted from other employees. She began directing others to do work "for the boss." Over time, resentment of her grew. They resented her attitude and her tone of voice when "asking" for help. Through the doorway, I could see this in their faces and their body language was screaming at me. I had a bit of a revolt in the making.

Because Evelyn was always going above and beyond in delivering what I needed, I didn't confront her about her behavior. But it worsened. So, when it came time for her annual evaluation, I delivered the message that I wasn't happy with how she interacted with the other staff and that it was having a negative impact upon morale.

Evelyn responded, rather incensed, "How long have you been concerned about this?" I replied, "Oh, about eight months." Now she really was upset. "You mean you have been disappointed in me all that time and never communicated it? Had I known I would have had a shot at correcting this before it became a problem. And, besides, those women need better supervision because they aren't delivering for this team and they should be called on it. I am doing all the work around here."

Well, she was right on all fronts. Indeed, she was performing at a level far above the others. Our relationship deteriorated for a considerable time. The work still got done, but there was a chill in the air. We weren't having fun. Ultimately, we weathered it. I fell on my sword and apologized for not being more honest with her, earlier. She deserved that from me.

Why This Matters

No doubt my failing caused considerable unhappiness, lowered motivation and performance with Evelyn. It also eroded already challenged teamwork as Evelyn resented others who had made known their displeasure with her. All of this could have been avoided. That's why immediate feedback matters.

Productive working relationships are both open and honest. Withholding feedback is in some ways a betrayal. The employee trusts that you are being open, honest and are committed to their success at the company. Withholding feedback until the annual evaluation erodes a trusting relationship.

The Annual Evaluation

I am not a fan of the annual evaluation process as normally practiced for numerous reasons. First, it is not frequent enough. Second, painted as objective, e.g., "your score is a 4 on a 1-5 scale", it is really subjective. You are rating all employees on a set of generic questions and not on how they performed on specific expectations and standards of their job. The evaluation is often tied to compensation changes which raises anxiety and takes the focus off performance improvement. The employee is waiting to hear about changes in compensation rather than working with you on a plan to improve performance.

If you are committed to making the journey with your employees to their full potential, then you have to ensure your relationship and relationships are built on improved communication/understanding. Annual evaluations as normally practiced are actually counter-productive to that end, especially if it is one of a few or the only one-on-one meetings that you have. Gallup (2020) found that only

14% of employees agree that performance reviews "inspire them to improve."

I believe there should be regular conversations around the 7 Questions, conducted no less than semi-annually, preferably monthly.

For companies that still require the annual evaluation, we recommend either replacing with a documented 7 Questions conversation and development plan or as a supplement to the evaluation form.

Going a step further, I have now made it my practice to give feedback on virtually every work product or client handling by my staff. I am specific on whether it met my standard or exceeded it and what it is that I particularly liked about it. If I feel it could have been done better then I communicate that as well.

Consider building competence and performance as if you were walking up a series of steps.. You take a step; you steady yourself and then you take the next step. Each step represents a new skill or a first-time independent action by the employee. In this metaphor, the supervisor encourages the employee to take the next step and then provides feedback on how it went along with any needed coaching in order to steady the risk taker on that new step.

As an example, I have developed a number of office managers/bookkeepers over the years. One of their responsibilities is to manage cash flow. When starting out, they have no clue about which bills need to be paid immediately, how much to hold in reserve, etc. Every two weeks we go through the exercise of looking at cash on hand, receivables due and payables and decide how to manage the cash. Then, I move to having the office manager prepare a set of recommendations based on how we have managed the cash in the past (first step). Ultimately, when they get to the top of the stairs, I am simply told what I am going to be paid this time around. This is an oversimplification, but you get the idea. Having invested the time early on, my time is now freed up forever more. It is the feedback on the recommendations that built confidence so the employee could act independently. Armed with that confidence, several office managers have gone on to start their own companies, which I consider a personal success.

It has consistently been both my experience and the experience of those whom I have taught that employees are relieved when you provide constructive criticism or feedback. Employees can sense if you aren't thrilled with them and they have already made the assumption that you judge them more harshly than you actually do. When feedback is provided, even if it is critical, they are relieved as the unknown is now known, and what is known is almost always more positive than what they feared.

On another note, no one wants to work for a manager who has low standards. People may criticize you for being demanding, but if you are demanding, and give them feedback and coaching as needed, they know they have earned something valuable that will serve them well throughout their career.

How to Get to "Yes"

Consider adopting these habits:

1. Examine each work product of your direct reports. A work product is a completion; a report, a new policy, revised process, marketing campaign, etc. Does that work product warrant feedback? Is it worthy of praise? Can you identify where it could have been improved? If yes, make note of it.

2. Deliver that feedback at the earliest convenience. These days, you are often copied on emails with work products

attached. Simply reply and provide the feedback. Invite the person to meet with you if there are questions. This response is quick, easy and immediate. It doesn't require a meeting or a phone call.

3. At least twice a year, have a formal meeting to provide general feedback. Go over the 7 Questions and identify areas to monitor for improved performance. At that time, make commitments on what steps you will take to help improve the employee's performance, e.g., coaching, investment in training, assigning a mentor and continuing regular feedback on work products.

4. If you do get a "yes" to this question, understand that there may be reluctance to give you a "no" when that is the truth. So, I would suggest probing a bit more with some follow up questions:

   - *Would you appreciate feedback more often?*

   - *Do you have clarity on what is particularly important to me?*

   - *Could my feedback be more precise to be actionable by you? Can you give me an instance in which I was not precise?*

   - *Are there areas of your performance that you are uncertain about whether you are meeting standards?*

When asking employees to answer Question #3, you are asking them if they understand whether they are doing a good job on an ongoing basis, not if they were clear on how you evaluated their performance six to twelve months ago. If the employees don't hear any feedback for months, doubt creeps into their minds about whether you remain satisfied with their work. Employees are reading your body language and tone of voice all the time to get a handle on your opinion. Instead of having them guess, communicate openly and frequently.

Question #4 – Authority

Jackie

Jackie had worked her way up in the group practice for years while demonstrating her loyalty to the owners and commitment to hard work. When personnel problems kept mounting, the owners decided to elevate Jackie to "manager." She now had taken on the responsibility for an office where backstabbing was the regular diet. What the owners failed to do was define and communicate to the staff the authority for her new responsibilities. Let me explain.

After months of frustration for both the owners and Jackie, I was brought in to help rectify the situation. I quickly assessed that Jackie was the "manager" in name only. She had no real authority. So, I started at the top, asking "Who is in charge?" The owners responded that they both were and that all decisions were made by consensus of the two owners. But they never met to make those decisions and instead delivered conflicting direction to Jackie and allowed staff to go directly to them for decisions undermining Jackie further.

Issues went unresolved. When Jackie was able to get their attention to ask for support of her authority and for consistent policy, the requests went unheeded. Worse, they blamed Jackie for problems in the office.

Employees would go to whichever owner they thought would be receptive and then that owner, without consulting the partner, would issue a decision. Decisions were inconsistent. In effect, there were no policies. The practice moved from crisis to crisis. With each decision by the owners, Jackie's effectiveness as "manager" was further undermined.

Jackie's authority was never established. Policies needed to justify her management actions were not put in place. The employees were working the owners for their own ends. Jackie found herself in tears and declining health. We had a real crisis here.

I met with the two owners and Jackie and got an agreement on a simple set of policies that Jackie would have the authority to enforce. I got a pledge from the owners that they would announce both the policies and Jackie's new authority at an all-staff meeting. I implored the owners to resist meeting with employees directly to hear their grievances and insisted that they work through Jackie. I also got a commitment that the owners would meet with Jackie regularly to assess the situation and solve problems together.

Well, too little too late. Jackie had already been undermined to the point that the situation couldn't be rehabilitated.

What Happened Here and Why This Matters?

The owners wanted nothing to do with day-to-day management. Their first commitment was to their patients. Managing the practice was a bother. They had no time for Jackie, but being good caregivers, always seemed to have time for the disgruntled employees working around her. Jackie was supposed to be responsible to create a problem-free office but she wasn't given the authority to make it happen.

Lacking faith and trust in her and always wanting to "be there" for employees, they simply made Jackie a buffer between the owners and the problems they didn't want to solve. The problems continued and Jackie's self-esteem eroded. It was cruel.

When I confronted the owners with my view of the situation, they were repentant. They wanted Jackie to succeed. They just didn't know how to make it happen. They did not understand trying to please all the employees was undermining her authority.

I have seen this happen at all levels of an organization. I worked with a CEO of a holding company in which the board was holding him accountable for subsidiary performance, but the subsidiary CEO's worked for independent subsidiary boards. After a few years of this, the holding company CEO finally stood up and said, "You can't hold me accountable for subsidiary performance because I have no authority over them."

Having sufficient authority is not just a function of what is defined in a job description or policy, but also in the leadership practice overseeing that position. If the judgment of a manager is always second-guessed or reversed and there is freedom for subordinates to go around the manager, then the manager has no real authority to get the needed results and expecting those results is fundamentally unfair.

Another common problem surrounds the authority to hire. That is, if a manager can't pick and/or terminate the members of a team expected to perform at a certain level, then it is unfair for the manager to be accountable for that level of performance.

A lack of sufficient authority leads to avoidance of responsibility rather than rising up to meet it. Rising up is challenging. It usually entails navigating uncharted waters. It triggers fear of failure. It's easier to justify not rising up because authority is lacking. Jackie, bless her heart, beat herself up instead. She was given an impossible mission and should have protested that from the beginning. However, she was loyal and grateful to the owners for supporting her start in the company and continuing her education.

Delegation of authority means letting go and trusting. Resist the tendency to review draft products or decisions once you have delegated. Be very explicit that you don't want to review the decision or product before it is implemented. And, that you understand there may be mistakes made but learning will come from them. It is common for employees to want to hedge their bets indefinitely by having you review draft products. But your goal should be to get them operating independently. In the short run, you may choose to provide coaching, but your goal should be to take the training wheels off as soon as possible.

How to Get to "Yes"

1. Just ask Question 4 and insist on an honest answer. Other ways to ask the question or to get into dialogue might be:

- *"Am I expecting something from you that you can't deliver?"*

- *"Are my own actions undermining your ability to get those results?"*

- *"What specific authority do you need from me to be able to accomplish what I am expecting?"*

2. With a new manager or someone in whom you don't have confidence, rather than pull back the authority, try increasing the level of coaching. Make it clear what decisions you want them to confer with you on. Then, make time for that to happen. Coach someone so the person is able to exercise authority independently as soon as possible. Having to confer with you on decisions means that someone is waiting for a decision, progress may be slowed and subordinates of your employee may be losing confidence in that supervisor.

Question #5 – Timely Decisions

One of the things Jackie tried to do to resolve her situation at the group practice was implement a set of personnel policies. She had been trying to accomplish this goal for some time but couldn't get the attention of the owners. I secured the commitment of the owners to do so.

Jackie completed research and delivered a set of draft policies to the owners for their approval. Jackie waited six months for a decision. She could not even get a meeting to discuss what she had proposed. Yet, the owners' expectation that she establish a problem-free work environment continued. This was an unfair expectation under a condition of no rules or boundaries. Their failure to decide prevented Jackie from achieving her potential.

You may be asking, "How could this be? How could you give someone responsibility, but then not provide either the authority for the person to make decisions or timely decisions." In fact, this happens all the time. A governing board might do this to a CEO or an owner to an office manager, which was the case with Jackie.

Why This Matters

Let's look at how this impacts performance. Suppose an owner expects the office manager to be sure that vendors are happy and that there is no interest expense due to late payments. Well, if the owner sits on the cash flow report and set of recommendations on the use of cash, then the office manager can't achieve that performance standard. A delay in decision-making would cause a delay in payment the bills and incurring of interest expense. Owner inaction makes the performance standard unfair. Accountability to an unfair standard is a recipe for high rates of turnover. People don't like playing a game they cannot win.

A common problem in this area is the time required to fill vacant positions due to process and decision-making time in HR and elsewhere.

Important to success here is defining "timely." Who defines the standard for "timely?" The answer is, "The person you are supervising." That person needs the decision when he or she needs it. If lack of decisions is slowing performance, they are untimely. Having a conversation on what "timely" looks like will inform you about the impact of delays. Knowing that, you can develop a plan to either deliver decisions when needed or expand the authority of your subordinate to make decisions.

How to Get to "Yes"

"Yes" would mean that the timing of your decision-making is not slowing performance. With Question 5, you are asking if more responsive decision-making would improve performance.

Couch the question in such a way that the employees don't feel like they are accusing you of being indecisive or slow. Rather, you are simply inquiring as to what impact the current practice of decision-making (could be by you, could be by your boss or could be by the board of directors) is having on performance.

Some suggested practices to help get to and maintain "yes" are as follows:

1. Regularly monitor what decisions are needed from you.

2. When asked to make a decision, ask directly when it is needed. After you agree upon when the decision will be made, make honoring that commitment a priority.

3. Recognize early on that if you don't have sufficient information and be specific in your request for additional information.

4. If you find subordinates bringing you decisions they should be making, ask them, "Have my previous leadership actions trained you to bring these decisions to me rather than make them yourself?" If the response is yes, then communicate that you believe the employee is ready to make the decisions and that not doing so is delaying progress and the person's own development. Encourage the employee that making a mistake is acceptable and that the worst that can happen is you both learn from it.

For the employee, giving you a "no" answer is a high risk. You will need to work hard to get the employee comfortable with being truthful. Be cautious so you don't get defensive. Also, understand that you may feel as if a decision was made, but the communication was such that it wasn't clear to the employee. Some follow-on questions might include:

- *Would more rapid decisions have made a difference? Which decisions?*

- *How did the delay impact you?*

- *Were the decisions untimely or incomplete/unclear? Which decisions?*

- *Were my requests for additional information reasonable and clear?*

Work toward a "yes," in simple steps that allow an employee to more easily state what he or she needs.

Question #6 – Resources

Matt

Matt was hired as the Director of Information Technology for a rapidly growing non-profit company with about 225 employees and more than twenty-five programs. Initially, despite a heavy backlog and a host of discouraged users, the job was relatively simple. It was basic PC support -- software updates, user education, updating machines and maintaining a relatively simple server system. Early on, any help was much appreciated by users. Matt was happy. Having waited so long for support to come along, users were willing to wait a bit longer to get real help. When the help arrived, Matt got accolades. Because of the backlog, he needed to clone himself to meet the demand, but he knew once he had done that, it would be clear sailing. He got approval for a new hire, made his clone and life was good.

But the organization continued rapid growth both in size and complexity. First, there was implementation of a complex billing system integrated across numerous programs. Then, there was the need to purchase, install and configure a phone system fully integrated with other systems. Looming on the horizon was the mandate for a new electronic medical record system serving several programs. The new record system needed substantial customization and would require reliance on outside vendors. All of this made Matt anxious. The pressures were becoming intense, indeed.

What initially was a satisfying job had become very frustrating. Matt was a man of high standards and integrity. He stood behind his systems. He was at the point where he lacked the personal bandwidth to maintain the current systems and prepare the organization for the future. Instead of being excited about the future and feeling appreciated, Matt was demoralized. He foresaw his personal standards at risk. He tried to caution management about the pace of change and lack of resources but was not successful. His previous success and management's confidence in him resulted in his cautions were falling on deaf ears.

Matt's contributions at management team meetings shifted from laying out what would be possible to protecting himself and his troops by limiting expectations of his department. His commitment to the purpose of the organization never wavered, but his production suffered. He began to complain about the lack of incentives for himself and his employees. "I can push them harder, but what's in it for them?"

Matt was caught in a dilemma. His choices were either to: 1) lower standards for himself and his staff to execute quick, but potentially unstable fixes, or 2) continue to push both himself and his staff for a level of production he considered unfair and risky. Matt didn't like either of the choices. He did not want himself associated with substandard work and he didn't want to be unfair in his expectations of his staff, especially when he didn't have authority to reward them for going beyond the normal call of duty.

Matt ultimately chose a third option. He left the organization which suffered as a result.

Why This Matters

The dilemma faced by Matt is common. It is found among the highly competent and committed. Superiors come to rely on such individuals. Expectations of them continue to rise. They are often asked to make up for the sub-standard performance of others. This may be fundamentally unfair but it is easier for supervisors than confronting the non-performance of others. Not wanting to let superiors or the organization down, the Matts of the world press on until they get to the point where their motivation and production is lost.

I have worked with both boards and individual leaders who use pushing subordinates to the breaking point as a means to find the limit of their productivity. The warnings of approaching the breaking point are ignored until it is too late. Getting the most from employees is a commendable goal but this technique of finding the end point is damaging.

Supervisors are always hearing that there is too much work and that more resources are needed. These are the cries of the 50-70 percent who have either inconsistent or low motivation. The challenge for supervisors is distinguishing the false cries for help from those that are truly overburdened. To do this, examine their productivity, their demonstrated commitment to the organization being all it can be and the data they put forth vs. complaints to make the case for more resources.

Alternatively, there is the risk associated with managers who consider asking for help to be a sign of weakness or failure and continue to press themselves and their staffs to the breaking point. Determining the truth compared to the appropriate level of resources is challenging. It should be data driven and assessed against best practices or peer organizations where possible.

Matt, if asked, might have suggested some combination of the following to solve his dilemma:

- Secure consulting help for evaluation and/or installation of new systems.
- Temporary authority to offer rewards to employees putting in extra time.
- Additional staffing.
- Some delay in the implementation of new systems.
- Potentially consulting help to define and implement methods that are more productive

But Matt was very self-reliant and had been burned by incompetent outside resources in the past. He saw turning to outsiders as a sign of failure. Thus, coming to agreement on a solution would be difficult.

Matt should have never been put in the position of having to decide between unacceptable alternatives. He was in that position because Question #6 had not been asked and addressed in a timely fashion.

The intent of Question #6 is to enable a manager to recognize the threat of a dilemma, like Matt's, before it is too late. "Too late," meaning there is a negative impact on motivation, morale and performance. Question #6, along with others, is intended to assess whether the "contract" (expectations and rewards) that you have with your employee is fair.

How to Get to Yes?

Getting an honest assessment on Question 6 is challenging. You don't want to make an offer of resources that is not needed. But you don't want stress on resources that erodes performance. You want lean but not starved. It's a fine balance.

The Matts of the world, i.e., the high achievers (until demoralized), don't like admitting that they can't get it done. They may reply, "I really appreciate you asking and your concern. I'm just having a bit of a bad day. I think we can get it under control here before too long." It is a matter of pride for these people that they are self-reliant and meet any challenges. You may need to explore a bit deeper to get to the truth and a real solution. The dialogue might go something like this:

Manager: *"Matt, from listening to you at our management team meetings, it appears that you are experiencing a high workload and stress within your department. True?"*

Matt: *"Yes, it has been tough lately. It seems like everything is coming all at once. There have been an unusual number of breakdowns. But we will get through it. I appreciate your asking."*

Manager: *"Well, it seems as if it has been going on for a while. Do you really see it letting up?"*

Matt: *"Yes, I think so. We just need to catch a break."*

Manager: *"OK. So, tell me more about the impact upon you, your troops and your outcomes from the current situation, since it has been going on for some time?"*

Matt: *"Well, I think the troops are a bit frustrated because they can't get ahead, and I am riding them hard all the time. We used to have a good time together, but now we all seem a bit testy."*

Manager: *"Understandable, but tell me what the impact is upon you?"*

Matt: *"Well, I'm just concerned that because we're moving so fast, I may be missing something. I would really like to have more time to understand and evaluate the new systems we are considering, but I don't feel right leaving all the day-to-day work to my staff because they are overloaded."*

Manager: *"Matt, I've been in situations like yours before. It wore on me, and I know it wears on you. I appreciate you wanting to take it all on yourself, but I also want to be sure we do these evaluations right and that you are confident that the new systems are going to work for us. Shouldn't we consider some alternatives to get us through this rough patch?"*

Matt: *"Well, I'm not sure I would trust anyone else to do the evaluations and bringing on new staff would just mean a further drag on me because I would have to train them up to do things right."*

Manager: *"I totally understand that Matt, but I also don't want the price of this to be burning out you or your staff or causing costly mistakes to be made because we are going too fast. Are there any tasks that we could trust an outside resource to handle for us? Maybe some low-level investigations of the experience other users have had with these new systems that would save you some time? Maybe contract some of the more basic PC support to an outside firm?"*

Matt: *"I'm not sure that is going to work, but I appreciate the offer."*

Manager: *"Do I need to scale back the expectations of your department, or delay some of these implementations?"*

Matt: *"I know how important these new systems are to our future and besides, some of these are mandated upon us. I don't think that is a solution."*

Manager: *"OK, but I would like you to give this further thought. I think we agree that the current situation is unworkable. I need you to define a workable solution and give me recommendations. Can we set up a time for you and I to meet after you have considered what might be helpful to get you out of this dilemma? I believe continuing on as we are would be too great a risk."*

Matt: *"I'm not sure I have time for that."*

Supervisor: *"Matt, I need you to make time for that. This situation is potentially dangerous. I don't want to lose you or to make costly mistakes. So, make the time to put together some proposals for me to consider. Now, when can we meet on this?"*

Sound familiar? It appears that Matt is going home and complaining to his wife about being overloaded by the unfairness of the situation. Matt is a ticking time bomb. So, in having conversations with a dedicated employee like Matt, you have to probe deeper and make it safe for the employee to receive help. Matt's instinctive reaction is to blame himself and view such a conversation as a sign of his own failure. The predictable response is to toughen up. But that rubber band will eventually break resulting in either Matt or his staff departing.

In this dialogue, the manager is seeing the truth behind Matt's body language and comments at management meetings. Quite correctly, the manager is choosing to confront these warning signs.

Once you know the reality of what is occurring, you can develop a plan of action to correct the situation. That plan of action might include additional short-term resources, as was the case for Matt. In the long-term, the solution for Matt would be better planning by the management team for future IT services, so that the needed resources are in place to execute projects.

A Word of Caution: Knowing Whether You Have the Right Resources

Take one note of caution on Question #6. When it comes to deciding whether there are sufficient resources, there is another consideration. Rarely do employees, when asked, state that they have enough time or resources to do what's expected of them. After all, if they did, the conclusion might be that they have a lot of spare time on their hands. Rather, a supervisor or CEO is always facing pressure at budget time to provide more resources in order to get the job done right. If a supervisor or CEO always accedes to this pressure, the company may become non-competitive due to excessive costs. Ideally, an organization should be lean and mean, which would mean that you may often hear that personnel are stretched thin. Lean and mean is good, but stretched too thin is not. How do know which is case?

How I Learned This Lesson

Early in my tenure building a rural health system, we took ownership of the small hospital in town. As I familiarized myself with the condition of the hospital as a whole and of each department, I became aware of a problem with delays in getting completed patient encounter forms into the patient medical record. Records were stacking up on the desk of the medical records supervisor waiting to be properly coded. When patients returned for follow-up visits, the records could not be located (this was some time ago when paper records were still being used), so physicians did not have access to information from previous visits, medications, etc. This was a potentially dangerous situation.

I confronted the medical records supervisor who had been there for years. She responded with a tale of woe about being overworked. "Understood," I said, "I will get you some help." I authorized another position for her department but the performance did not improve. So, I authorized another position but there was still no change. Finally, a third position was added but the result was the same.. Each time my conversation with the supervisor was a repeat of the story about her being overworked.

Ultimately, I came to the conclusion that resources were not lacking but organizational and supervisory skills were. Ultimately, we mutually agreed to part ways.

I recruited a new medical records supervisor fresh out of a graduate program. In less than six months, not only had she eliminated the backlog, but implemented an entirely new record system and did so without filling some vacancies in her department. And, she was in my office complaining about being bored.

The moral of the story is that a "no" answer to Question 6 should signal the need for an evaluation of the quality of supervision and work processes to determine the root cause of the backlog. It should not signal an automatic adding of resources.

How to Get to the Truth

Areas of investigation to determine the root cause might include the following:

- How well are employees under the supervisor being oriented, trained and utilized? Do they have "yes's" to the 7 Questions?

- Are the existing processes within the department undermining the ability of employees to be productive?

- How does the ratio of employees to output compare with peers (if such data is available)?

Should you get a "no" answer to Question 6 regarding resources, then you need to continue the dialogue to get clarity here. Some follow-on questions might be the following:

- *Is it a particular expertise that is lacking?*
- *Is this the result of someone in the group not meeting standards?*
- *Is the workload evenly balanced across your team?*
- *What are the indicators that the workload is unrealistic? Do you have peer organizational data to support the need for additional resources?*
- *Are there ways in which processes or methods could be streamlined, so that more could be accomplished with the resources we have?*
- *Is the root cause lack of cooperation from other departments, delays, etc.?*
- *What data is missing and how would it be used?*
- *What was the impact of the lack of support?*
- *What are the instances in which support was lacking?*
- *What would the needed support have looked like?*
- *Would the solution involve more resources or more recognition and credit for better results?*
- *What would a solution look like to you?*

Once the root causes have been determined, you and the supervisor can develop a plan of action to correct the situation. The plan of action might include short-term additional resources as in the case for Matt and his IT department. It may also be improving the ability of the supervisor to streamline processes and gain better productivity from employees through your coaching or outside assistance.

Question #7 – Credit

Dave

Dave had worked for Interior Air for nearly fifteen years. Although not a member of the family that owned the business, Dave felt part of the family. He had joined the second generation of family owners and other friends as part of the transition. The company had grown rapidly and had been consistently successful. Dave was an integral part of the meteoric rise of the company and felt that his contributions were appreciated.

Initially, Dave was responsible for accounting and oversaw most administrative functions. Having stabilized those operations, he took on the challenge of building the information technology systems that would give Interior an advantage over its competitors. He had personally written the code for an innovative package tracking system that performed much like that of FedEx. None of Interior's competitors had anything like this system.

In short, Dave was highly responsible and met every challenge given him. As the organization grew, Dave was often the only one with the courage to speak truthfully about problems. This trait should have been invaluable, but Interior's leadership was obsessed with growth and didn't want to hear about or address these problems. Furthermore, the management team could not see the potential of taking advantage of Dave's package tracking system to achieve competitive advantage. Leadership was pilot-centric. Slowly, but surely, Dave was becoming dispirited while his contributions to discussion of strategy and priorities were being marginalized. He no longer felt the appreciation and satisfaction he once did. No one recognized his waning enthusiasm.

At about the same time, it became apparent that the CEO was spread too thin. He was trying to juggle strategizing and executing growth initiatives, overseeing operations, performing check rides on pilots as well as filling in when pilots were out ill or on vacation. That portfolio was not sustainable. Unless this issue was fixed, the rapid growth of Interior would stall out.

I was working with the CEO on revising the organizational structure and suggested that Dave be approached about assuming more management responsibilities and finding someone to take over his IT duties. I was given a green light to approach Dave with the idea.

The conversation set me back and taught me a valuable lesson.

Dave's response went something like this:

"Why would I want to bail him out I have enough pressures already. There's nothing in it for me to take on those pressures."

There were two forces at play here. On the one hand, there was resentment that the CEO was not meeting the needs of the organization for leadership and decision-making. On the other hand, Dave wasn't getting enough credit for what he was contributing. So, he couldn't justify committing to contributing more. Had Dave gotten his due credit for his past contributions, this conversation might have gone differently.

Why This Matters

Dave, like Matt in the previous chapter, was a peak performer. Peak performers are often saddled with taking on the tough challenges that others aren't willing to assume. Over time, they often feel taken advantage of. They're not likely to easily admit to feeling this way but may do so when asked directly if they have received sufficient credit for past results.

Again, using the rubber band analogy, employees like Dave and Matt can be stretched very thin, so that the band can snap quickly and unexpectedly. Once it does, it is difficult to repair.

Therefore, Question 7 matters because it can uncover a hidden risk factor. This is a risk that will not surface unless you have a very acute sense for the warning signs, e.g., less participation in meetings, rolling the eyes in management team meetings, less humor and withdrawal. Again, this question when presented properly can unearth what is difficult to get at.

How to Get to "Yes"

What influences whether or not a subordinate will answer "yes?" Here are some factors to investigate as you dialogue with them:

- *Have their contributions been acknowledged and appreciated?*

- *Given how they have performed relative to their peers, do they feel as if they have been taken advantage of?*

- *Do they see others being held accountable to perform at the same level?*

- *Has public recognition in the form of compensation, promotions etc. been fair in relation to others?*

In our story, Dave had reached the end of the line. He was no longer willing to extend himself to aid the CEO or the company because he felt he was being taken advantage of.

You might begin the conversation on this question by admitting that you don't always take the time to appreciate the efforts of those contributing to making you and the company successful. Express clearly that there have been times when you have felt taken advantage of yourself and you don't want others to experience that. By starting this way, you begin by accusing yourself rather than leaving it to the employee to accuse you of being unfair. The employee is only affirming what you already are anxious about. This will work only if such statements from you are true and sincere.

This type of opening can create an entry point for honest dialogue. It is our nature to want to be appreciated. Not feeling appreciated impacts motivation and, in turn, performance. The ability to get to "yes" is important for strengthening job satisfaction.

The rest of the conversation with Dave might have gone as follows:

Manager: Dave, I'm particularly interested in whether you feel as if you have been given due credit for the results that you have produced. Much was accomplished before I joined the company. I know you contributed a great deal to that success. So, do you feel that you were given due credit for those results?

Dave: It's been all right. Lots of us contributed. It was a team effort.

Manager: OK. I appreciate that but feeling as if you got credit for results is a personal thing. What's your own calculation in regard to this question? Has the company been appreciative and fair to you?

Dave: *Well, not really.*

Manager: *Thanks. As you see it, what should have happened either on my watch or before I came back?*

Dave: *To be truthful, I felt that I should have been given a bigger raise when I took on overseeing all administrative functions. Not getting that was one reason why I wanted to give it up.*

Manager: *I can see that. What about since you have been overseeing IT? I know you have made great strides there.*

Dave: *Well, I see my developing the package tracking software as having saved us a bunch of money and given us a huge competitive advantage. I thought I should have been received some company stock for that contribution.*

Manager: *All right. I really appreciate you being honest with me. I know it was difficult. I need to give this some consideration. My commitment to you is that we come to an agreement that seems fair to both of us. Let me give this some thought and get back to you.*

For Dave, such a conversation might have been too little, too late. Dave had become a "Won't Do" employee with regard to taking on additional responsibilities. He was doing well on what was expected of him now. The "Won't Do" was associated with considerations about contributing more. His viewpoint might change over time if he were to feel more appreciated. But for now, with his sense of fairness having been violated, it was a very tough sell.

As with some of the previous questions, a truthful answer may be hard to secure. The employee may think that humility is the best course here. Some additional questions to continue the dialogue would be the following:

- *"Do you feel as if your efforts are appreciated?"*

- *"Am I or others taking credit where credit should be given to you?"*

- *"Looking at your contributions relative to your peers and to the credit they have received, have we been fair with you?"*

- *"Is there anything that would increase your motivation to contribute here?"*

Getting to a "yes" on this question is not just about "attaboys." That is, credit may mean more than recognition. It may even involve compensation.

The 7 Questions — Key Points

1. Prepare your reasons explaining why you are changing the nature of meeting with employees and the goal for the conversation before asking the Questions.

2. Don't rely on glib or rapid "yes's." Make clear such answers give you no room to be of help.

3. If necessary, go through the Questions several times or in a follow-up meeting.

4. #1 – Making Expectations Clear - Do not rely on job descriptions. Make priorities clear. Lack of clarity leads to caution and low performance

5. #2 – Communicate Performance Standards including the hidden pet peeves that aren't detailed in a job description. Create a clear picture of the ideal product/service and communicate it.

6. #3 – Give Feedback. This monitors whether you are giving ongoing feedback about whether employee results are

matching your standards. The more frequent the feedback, the greater the chance for improvement. Withholding comments until the annual evaluation erodes a trusting relationship.

7. #4 – Appropriate Authority – Being accountable for performance without the authority to direct and take corrective actions is unworkable and fundamentally unfair.

8. #5 – Timely Decisions – If performance is negatively impacted by having to wait for decisions/approvals, then decision making is untimely. Being accountable for performance unachievable because decisions are lacking is unfair. Would performance improve if decisions were made timelier?

9. #6 – Adequate Resources – Lack of resources results in unfair expectations, ultimately defeating morale and performance. It is essential to distinguish between false cries for help of the incompetent from genuine unrealistic expectations.

10. #7 – Give Credit – At its core, this is about a sense of appreciation for one's efforts. It may or may not be monetary. Without employees getting it, they will continue to feel as if they are giving more than receiving which wears on motivation and ultimately performance.

6.

The Performance Context

The 7 Questions need to be asked in the context of the employee's current level of performance. Introducing the new role of coach committed to the employee achieving full potential begs the question, "where am I in terms of potential right now?" The questions are intended to unearth the reasons underlying why the employee is falling short of potential. The responses are intended to form the content of an action plan to achieve full potential.

Without the context of current performance and with an employee assumption that his or her current performance is fine, it becomes easy to offer a glib "yes" to all the Questions. This leaves the supervisor with no definable path to add value to the employee or organization.

So, after explaining the shift in role to coach and to a change in format of your meetings, state something like the following:

> *"To get us started on a road to reach your full potential at work, let me give you my assessment of your performance with regard to what is expected of you currently.*

Then, we can move to a plan to either improve that performance or to begin adding new skills and experience to prepare you for the next step in your career. I am going to lay out each of your current responsibilities in terms of results expected and then your performance on each. I will put performance on each responsibility in one of three buckets: Exceeds Expectations, Meets Expectations, Below Expectations. Then, we can discuss specifics and where we go from here."

In the appendix you will find a sample form you can use to document your conversation.

When defining the current responsibilities, the existing job description may be helpful but it is recommended that you reword them to accountabilities. Job descriptions tend to be stated in terms of "To Do's." For clarity, change the wording to define results. Below are some examples:

To Do's	Results
Prepare billing slips	Billing slips completed accurately and on-time
Prepare project budgets and proposals	Project budgets and proposals completed and submitted to prospective client
Orient new hires	New hires fully oriented and prepared to perform their duties
Administer medications	All medications administered accurately, on-time and documented in medical record

The intent of the change is to gain clarity and also to state responsibilities in terms of completion rather than effort. Accountability for results is much tighter and more effective than accountability for effort.

Having laid out current performance, the conversation can now shift to uncovering the reasons why expectations are not being exceeded. Is there lack of clarity on expectations or standards? Lack of skill? Lack of confidence? Lack of motivation? Lack of needed resources/support? A shift in the personal life of the employee? Remember, your intent here is to define areas where your actions can help the employee achieve a better performance. The traditional employee evaluation puts the onus on the employee to get his act together. Here, the emphasis is on defining the steps a coach can take to build a better player. The action plan will include interim standards or milestones (performance goals), but unless your conversation uncovers that you truly have a Won't Do situation, then the first elements of the action plan need to be actions you will take to fill in the employee's gaps or help build confidence to act independently.

For employees currently exceeding all expectations, the conversation should shift to defining future career goals and desired new skills/experience. The action plan then becomes how you can provide the training, coaching, and support to achieve those new goals and lay out opportunities for the employee to try completing tasks in the new area.

The Performance Context — Key Points

1. Newfound honesty in your relationship begins with honest assessment of the employee's current performance.

2. You can't add value if you haven't defined the gap between current and potential performance.

3. State existing accountabilities in terms of results.

4. Put performance on each accountability in one of three categories: Exceeds, Meets, Below Expectations.

5. Then, employ the 7 Questions to define what is missing and how to fill the gaps.

7.

Relationship and The Underlying Principle of Fairness

Relationship is defined as a condition of being connected. That's actually not very helpful. The easiest way to understand it is that when in a relationship, what happens to someone else, happens on some level to you. They win, you win. They are happy, you are. When they fail, on some level, so do you.

The new role in managing people calls for moving to a coach or, better yet, a partner (*def: one that is united or associated with another in an activity or sphere of common interest*) in realizing the potential of employees, the organization, and the leader. The quality of relationship required is much higher than that of the traditional supervisor or overseer. Overseer is a one-way relationship with the supervisor having minimal responsibility to employee. At its core, the exchange in the relationship is compensation in exchange for adequate work.

Partnership is a more co-equal, two-way relationship. Each party has accountability to the other and has a legitimate role in holding to agreements made. The manager is accountable to deliver what is needed for employee development and success. The employee is accountable to deliver on agreed-upon performance goals subject to delivery of what is needed by the manager.

The 7 Question conversation involves each partner communicating whether commitments have been met. There is a shift from one-way to two-way accountability.

Moving to a deeper relationship involves several key factors, including:

1. caring for one another

2. being honest and trustworthy

3. the ability to understand one another

4. the level of agreement about the world around us

5. fairness of exchange

Relationships are deepened and strengthened by improving the quality and depth of communication to gain mutual understanding on these factors.

Agreeing that the relationship remains fair is the key to continued success of the partnership.

Fair: def. – being in accordance with relative merit or significance.

Exchange: def. – to give in return for something received.

Think of your own marriage or those that you have observed. What are the root causes of most arguments? Do they not often lie in fairness of exchange, i.e., whether or not the parties are doing their "fair share"? It can be about chores, earning/spending money or raising children. When one party feels that the exchange is no longer fair, the disagreements begin and the relationship erodes.

I had a successful business partnership for more than three decades. Did we have differences? Of course. But we maintained commitment to being fair to one another and respected each other's view on fairness. When the relative contribution to the business was considered to have shifted, we would always talk about and modify our partnership agreement if needed. We made such adjustments numerous times over the years as our roles in the business changed. Once the adjustments were made, we could turn our attention to improving our products, designing new ones and collaborating on meeting client needs. We didn't harbor resentments. We didn't avoid one another. The times we let perceived unfair exchange go on too long, we stopped communicating, stopped collaborating and, ultimately, stopped producing as a partnership. Instead, we continued on in our own little world with our clients while harboring unexpressed resentment.

There is no objective formula for determining fairness. Everyone has their own consideration on the value they are providing relative to the value they are receiving. The only way to keep the relationship healthy and productive is regular dialogue on whether it still feels fair or to agree that the moment it doesn't that you will talk about it. While it isn't easy to appreciate another's point of view on the value of your work, harboring resentment is a heavy and corrosive burden.

You cannot achieve employee engagement unless fairness is maintained.

Let's look at the 7 Questions and how they pertain to fairness of exchange:

1. *Do you know what is expected of you?*

2. *Do you know what good performance looks like in your job as defined by your supervisor?*

3. *Do you get feedback on the results that you produce?*

4. *Do you have sufficient authority to carry out your responsibilities?*

5. *Do you have the data, resources and support needed to meet what is expected of you?*

6. *Do you get timely decisions in the areas where you don't have authority?*

7. *Do you get credit for the good results that you produce?*

Questions #1-3 are designed to support the employee delivering needed results. It is unfair to expect certain results without making clear what those results should be. Doing so would likely prompt the response, "How can you make me wrong for not doing what I didn't know I was supposed to be doing in the first place?" This is why Questions #1 & 2 are so important.

It is also unfair to have employees wondering whether they have met your standards or not. If you don't provide ongoing feedback and instead wait until the annual evaluation, as I did with my executive secretary Evelyn, you will likely get an irritated response along the lines of, "Why didn't you tell me sooner, so I could have corrected this?" Again, this situation is fundamentally unfair. This is why Question #3 is vital.

Not taking action to assure a "yes" answer to these questions will lead to a sense of unfairness. You may be saying that you see the relationship as a partnership to get to the employee's full potential, but you are not meeting your end of the bargain. The employee can't deliver what you expect because you haven't provided what is needed to make that happen. Over time, resentment will build, communication will break down, production will not be acceptable and the relationship will be under serious threat. This explains disengagement of employees and why "bad bosses" is the number one reason for unwanted turnover.

Alternatively, look at successful athletic coaches. They are in the faces of their players when they don't perform, communicating in the moment what they failed to do and challenging them to correct. They don't simply pull the player and have them sitting on the bench wondering "why did I get pulled?" Then, they coach them on needed corrections and put them back in the game.

Questions #4, #5 & #6 verify whether expectations are fair under current conditions. Are needed authority, resources and decisions in place or is the employee prevented from success or full potential because they are lacking?

Examples: It is not fair to hold people accountable for the performance of their team when they don't have authority to hire and fire that team. It is not fair to expect someone to meet a production goal without resources needed to meet that goal. It is unfair to expect deadlines to be met when employees have to wait for needed decisions.

Question #7 regarding credit for good results also impacts perceived fairness. Is someone else getting credit for an employee's results? Is there fairness in the salary and bonus structure?

Are peak performers given due credit? Are the workloads fairly distributed or is there overreliance on peak performers?

Considerations of fairness are an evaluation of the "contract" between the organization and the employee. As manager, you are the administrator of that contract. Even if you don't have authority to define the terms (e.g., salary structure or decision making authority), you do have influence over them and you can advocate for fairness, ramp up non-financial appreciation or adjust expectations if unfair.

An honest "yes" to all 7 Questions signals that fairness likely exists. If not, then you need to continue to work your way to "yes" through honest dialogue on what's missing and what would fill the void. You can also add a direct question about fairness.

Examine Your Own Beliefs About Fairness

Think about situations in which you were uncomfortable because you weren't doing your fair share. Say, someone else does all the work, but you get all the credit. Or a friend is always reaching out to help you or always picking up the tab. Do you feel that you need to even the score with them? Do you feel uncomfortable when indebted? Hopefully, the answer is, "yes."

Now, look at how you view your employees. Do you see them as trying to take advantage of you or the organization? Are they trying to get something for nothing? Well, is that really true? How do you know that? And do you view them as having a different attitude about fairness than yourself? Do the views of management as a whole differ from your own on this question? How is the organization doing in terms of fairness with its employees? How does fairness in the organization impact the organizational culture and employee engagement?

Employees and their unions often push for more compensation and more benefits. Are their requests unfair? Or are they asking because they have not been treated fairly?

The history of unions includes challenging business barons who inflicted unfair working conditions and compensation. The employees were simply seeking fairness. Are they fighting for fairness today or are their demands unfair? Are they willing to be fair partners when times are tough in exchange for fairness when the organization is prospering?

Why Fairness Matters

My own experience is that when you are fair with employees, they feel an obligation to maintain their end of the bargain. It is the commitment to fairness and the expressions of appreciation of their work that has the biggest impact upon their engagement.

Alternatively, employees sensing a lack of commitment to fairness and observing benefits accruing largely to those in management will build resentment and lose commitment.

Won't Do Employees and Fairness

One of the characteristics of Won't Do employees is that they have a somewhat skewed view on fairness. They may lack an innate sense of fairness and be comfortable taking something for nothing. Despite not actually producing, they project a high level of commitment, complain of being overworked and boast about their contributions and importance. They often are lobbying for more compensation on the grounds that they are carrying their team when in reality the opposite is true.

There are two words of caution here. Don't take a "no" response to Question #7 regarding "credit for results" at face value. Examine actual data before determining that this "no" response warrants action on your part. What data? Well, what are the actual results produced? How do those results compare with that of others doing similar work? How does the compensation compare with those producing work at the same level? If the employee cites salaries from competitors, then secure verification of that data.

Determine Where You Are and Strengthen the Partnership with Employees

I raise the issue of fairness so that you can examine your own views on the matter and how those views are impacting your success in developing employees.

The 7 Questions determine whether there is fairness between manager/organization and the employee. They examine whether the "contract" is fair. A "no" response to any of the questions may mean it is not so. In the previous chapters, I recommended some follow-on questions that can clarify the true condition of the "partnership" and what you need to do to strengthen it. A good follow-on question for each of the 7 Questions would focus on fairness. That is, you might get a "yes" on clear expectations, feedback, credit etc. but still have a perception of unfairness. Ask the question and if the employee indicates a sense of unfairness, find out why and come to your own judgment, i.e., are expectations excessive, standards unfair, resources lacking, credit for results insufficient. Then, propose changes to strengthen the partnership.

Relationship and The Underlying Principle of Fairness — Key Points

1. Success in developing employee potential means moving your relationship from overseer to partner, from one-way accountability to two-way accountability to deliver on agreements made.

2. Mutual agreement on the fairness of the "contract" between organization and employee is needed for motivation for the employee to achieve full potential contribution to the organization

3. Fairness is both objective and subjective. Dialogue is required to assure that it exists.

4. Each of the 7 Questions touches on an aspect of the "contract." For each you can ask whether fairness exists or ask a general question about overall fairness in the organization's and your relationship with the employee.

5. Fairness includes whether evaluation of performance is timely and objective.

6. "Won't Do" employees may have unrealistic views on fairness as they refute their failure to produce.

8.

Putting the 7 Questions to Work

Managers spend somewhere between 40% and 80% of their time managing others (the time varies by how much actual production is required of them and how many individuals they are supervising). The balance of their time is spend doing technical work, i.e. producing results for the organization themselves results themselves (technical work). The higher the management level, the higher percentage of management work. Management work, by definition, does not directly contribute to the results of the organization. That is, you aren't producing a product or serving an external customer. Rather, you add value by improving the performance of those working with you. If, in a given year, the performance of your team has not improved, then the cost of your position is taking from the bottom line, not adding to it.

Your job as manager is to get a genuine "yes" response to all 7 Questions. A genuine "yes" means that you have delivered what is needed rather than the employee having to figure it out for his/herself or go without needed support. If you don't get a "yes," then you need to continue dialogue to gain clarity on what specific actions are needed by you to get to a "yes" and develop a plan of action to deliver it.

How You Can Add Value

Responses to the 7 Questions and dialogue about what is missing, should lead to a clear detailed plan for improved performance that details actions by the manager and performance benchmarks for employee. It may be daunting for the employee to be truthful about what they need as it pinpoints deficiencies. The Questions will help focus on specifics.

Be cautious of glib "yes" responses. The employee should understand that all "yeses" would mean that there is no barrier to exceeding expectations other than barriers they own. Understanding this may prompt more truthful responses. Make clear that there will be no retribution for pointing out what's missing. Quite the contrary, it will define a path for you to add value.

Applications of the 7 Questions

There are six ways in which the 7 Questions can play a valuable role:

1. Improving the onboarding of new employees

2. Improving management practice

3. Evaluating performance

4. Assuring fairness

5. Determining the proper course of action for an underperforming employee

6. Increasing employee engagement

1. Improving Onboarding of New Employees

By "onboarding," I mean the process of setting an employee up for early success. It is more than a tour of the office or facility, introductions, and highlighting portions of the employee manual. It includes providing the direction, training, feedback and support to minimize learning by mistakes. It requires planning and persistence by the manager. HR may initiate some elements of the process but the manager must assure that it has been effective and fill in any gaps.

Most organizations don't commit sufficient resources to this effort. If you have ever observed or experienced this being done effectively, then you know the return on investment that comes from it. One organization I am familiar with puts all their new employees through a multi-week program before they begin seeing clients. The purpose is to instill the strong values and operating principles of the organization, build teaming skills and so on. By the end of the program, both the organization and the employee are clear on whether there is a fit and if future success is likely.

It falls to the manager to orient a new employee to the specifics of their position. The following are the challenges to doing this successfully:

1. Lack of Time

The manager must balance continuing demands to do technical work, manage the workload of the team, solve problems and somehow find time for on boarding and development of individuals. Often, this is unrealistic as demands for technical work are not reduced. Contributing to this is failure to develop and delegate, thus it becomes a self-fulfilling prophecy. Setting aside major blocks of time for orientation is often overlooked as it lacks the urgency of the phone messages, emails, meetings and the like. Managers tend to look at the prior experience of the incoming employees and make the assumption that they know what to do. The cure for this deficiency is to acknowledge the importance and potential return on investment of time and simply block out the time on your calendar to do it right. Ask yourself, what is more important than doing all that I can to get this new employee off on the right foot? The press of the day to day will always be there. In fact, it will increase if you don't position new employees for success. The world does not fall apart when you are on vacation and won't if you devote multiple several hour blocks to doing this well.

2. Lack of Planning and Preparation

In order to save time and have positive results, plan out the on-boarding rather than doing it on the fly. It makes sense to design a usable plan and prepared materials that can be applied to each new employee. Contents, logical order, needed documents, needed coaching/ mentoring, time with other employees, and checklists should all be devised thoughtfully. To start the design, ask yourself or someone else, what would you have wanted to know when you started that you didn't know?

3. Inability to be Highly Directive

My failure with David, the new clinic manager, was due to both #1 and #2 above but also to not wanting to insult him by assuming he didn't know. Faulty logic. Don't assume. At worst, ask the question about whether new employee is certain. Better yet, go over it anyway. Doing so will reveal the little things, your hidden standards, that are important to you. This will assure you are not judging later on what you didn't make clear in the beginning.

4. Addiction to Doing Technical Work

Finding satisfaction in producing the results the department/team needs vs. developing others to be more productive is a common problem. You are good at it. Being good at it is why you got selected to manage. Doing what you do well is satisfying. Managing, not something that you do well or even like doing, takes a back seat to the addiction of doing what we love, do easily, do well and that produces immediate results/gratification. This all feeds the self-perception that there is not enough time.

If these challenges seem familiar to you, then I suggest beginning the onboarding with this disclosure:

> *"I need to forewarn you that I have a history of not doing well starting employees off on a sound footing for success. I simply don't take the time or go into the necessary detail in orienting to what is expected, what my standard for good performance is, what the relevant policies are and so on. I don't want to make that mistake with you. So, if I go into too much detail or cover something that you already know then I don't mean to insult your intelligence. I am just making sure that I don't make the mistakes I have made previously. If I don't cover something that you have questions about, please stop me and ask them. Most important, I want to set you up for early success to the extent possible."*

After the first few days of on boarding or "hatting," Questions 1, 2 and possibly 4 & 5 are appropriate to ask. Give the employee the full list of Questions and communicate that you are going to want answers to the additional questions in the near future. You want to know if the on boarding was complete. Decide together at what future point, such as thirty, sixty or ninety days into the employee's tenure, you will revisit the Questions. The shorter the waiting period, the better. Making certain employees have what they need to be successful ensures that they get "wins" or positive feedback early, which is key to engagement and retention.

Having completed hundreds of organizational assessments, it is clear that inadequate employee on boarding is frequently an issue. Commitment of resources to do it well is rare. If this rings true for you, then advocate for greater commitment to this process within your organization.

2. Improving Management Practice

Be mindful, if your employees are not improving performance, then your management can be improved. Lack of time (or more accurately not making it a priority) is a principal reason managers underperform for their employees. The 7 Questions enable conversations to get to the heart of the matter and create a targeted action plan for improvement by both parties. Efficiency of managers should dramatically improve. The quicker you get employees to certain "yeses" on the 7 Questions, the less time you will need to spend solving problems, correcting mistakes and monitoring. By instituting effective control, you enable employees to be in control and empowered. To a large degree, the ship will run itself.

Let's examine how each question might lead to improved management practice:

1. Do You Know What's Expected of You?

A "no" response here could be the result of any of the following:

- Job description is unclear. It may be describing activities, but not the expected outcomes.

- Measures of success aren't defined.

- Priorities are unclear. It could be that you have sent verbal signals that create confusion about what is important.

- Accountabilities in special projects are not specified

- Authorities for decision-making are not defined.

- Conflicting direction has come from one or multiple sources.

- The same assignments have been given to multiple individuals.

- There is lack of clarity regarding who is team leader on projects involving a team.

- Policies are unclear or inconsistently applied.

If you get a "no," "sometimes," or "unsure," then begin the dialogue with "what's missing?" or "what's unclear?" You need to be careful here. You may believe you have been very clear or you may somehow signal that you are offended when told that you have not been. Your body language can cause the employee to cease being truthful. Listen carefully. Get a precise definition of what's missing. Generalities in the employee's responses here are a potential indicator of a "Won't Do" situation. I'll discuss this more in Chapter 9. Lastly, thank the employee for being honest and contributing to making this go better for both of you.

Develop an action plan for correction. List the specific steps you need to take, prioritize them and commit to a date at which point you will have delivered the correction. Then, check to be sure that is the case in a scheduled follow-up. Do this jointly with the employee, review the final action plan with him/her and then deliver a copy. Include in the action plan a specific date for check in on progress.

2. Do You Know What Good Performance Looks Like?

Have you created a clear picture of excellent performance on expectations? These are your standards which are rarely found in job descriptions. Your experience has created a list of items in your mind that particularly please or annoy you in the results produced. What are those? Make them clear to your subordinate. Use personal stories to relate how you came to these standards. Think about the best and worst employee you have had in a given role. The descriptors define your standards. Before the game begins, make known what a homerun looks like in your eyes. It's only fair.

Remember the story about JoAnn, the office manager/consultant who was shocked to learn that excellence for me meant staying on the phone and being there for the customer rather than getting off as soon as possible? Be proactive; communicate these standards during orientation so the employee knows the appropriate behavior from the start. Hidden standards pulled out at a later date to make the employee seem ineffective will only cause problems in the future that are hard to recover from.

3. Do You Get Feedback on the Results You Produce?

A "yes" would mean your feedback has been specific, frequent and includes both positive and negative comments. "Good job" simply doesn't get it. What was good about it? Or what would it have taken to hear "great job?"

If you only provide feedback that is positive, the employee is going to wonder whether they are getting true or complete feedback. If you have previously communicated something like, "This was good, but would have been improved if ....," then when you do give unbridled positive feedback it is considered genuine.

Most employees are harder on themselves than you will be. Shed your reluctance to give negative feedback and commit to move to a fully honest and open relationship. Employees know when they are not performing well or up to their potential. And they can see that you know. They just aren't certain how negatively you judge their performance. Your feedback is almost certain to be good news relative to what they fear you will say.

You may also want to dialogue on whether your standards are reasonable or even correct. The customer for the employee's production (if someone other than you) may have told the employee that they want something else. Let's take the example of how JoAnn handled customer communications. There could be instances in which the customer has said, "I don't have time for chit chat. Just answer my questions as quickly as possible." The employee may have a better handle on shifts in customer needs and wants than you do. Be open to hearing what your employee is hearing from the customer. What gets praise and what gets criticism?

Lastly, feedback is an ongoing occurrence, not an annual event. Evaluations or performance discussions should be done AT LEAST semi-annually and informal feedback should be provided regularly. When you receive a work product from a direct report, give the employee feedback at that time. Was it great? What would you suggest in the future that would make it even better? No feedback means you are not even acknowledging that the product is complete. This creates doubt about whether the product matters or was worth the effort. In today's work environment, emails or texts providing feedback can be sent quickly and easily.

Be comfortable asking by what method and how frequently feedback is desired. In some cases, high performers don't need it or want to be bothered with it. Such conversation is all about building relationship and tailoring your actions to the needs of employees.

4. Do You Have Sufficient Authority to Carry Out Your Responsibilities?

Imagine being a carpenter trying to meet expectations but not having the tools. Such are the seeds that sow resentment. This Question as well as two that follow examine whether employees have what they need to produce what is expected, whether the "contract" is fair. Authorities needed might include authority to hire and fire, to reprimand, to purchase, to contract, to set policy or to change process design. The more that can be safely delegated, the more self-determined and responsible the employee can be and the fairer high standards will be considered.

Some follow-on questions that address fairness directly are the following:

- Are expectations of you clear given your existing level of authority?

- How is limited authority impacting performance, if at all?

The action plan for correction on this question might include steps for you to gain confidence in delegating decision making. For example, you might ask for input on a decision you are making and examine the quality of the rationale provided. Coach as needed to move to confidence in delegating the authority needed if you agree that is where you should go. In any case, address the fairness question by either changing authorities or expectations.

5. Do you get timely decisions in the areas where you don't have authority?

Lack of authority (Question #4) usually means a waiting period for needed decisions. Delays may suppress performance and motivation. Thus, important to discuss.

If the answer is "no" or "sometimes," then specifically explain how this impacts performance.

The action plan might include your commitment to turn around decisions in a certain timeframe, asking the employee to provide better information when requesting a decision or lobbying for your own decision-making authority to be expanded so that you can delegate.

What's important is that you do not want this to be the bottleneck impeding performance.

6. Do you have the data, resources and support needed to meet what is expected of you?

This question is rather straightforward. If you get a "no," then a good follow-on question might be, "What additional information, resources or support would have enabled you to be more productive and successful?"

Repeating my previous word of caution, there is always pressure for more resources. I have rarely encountered a situation in which someone says, "I have all the employees and resources that I need." The pressure to increase budgets is constant. The ideal situation is a lean organization that is running resources hard, but not too hard. It is a tough line to walk. Organizations that are fat become lethargic and don't perform well. Organizations that are too lean tend to create stress and burnout their employees. Finding the right mix of resources and expectations is challenging.

It is important to remember that one of the maxims of W. Edwards Deming was that he never found a situation where there was less than 25 percent waste (defined as any process step, task or expense that did not add value to the end product in the minds of the customer). That is certainly, true in my experience. Ask yourself and the employee, are the methods we are employing optimal? Are there instances where production slows waiting for resources, decisions, help from another department, etc.? Explore this in depth. You may want to invest in teaching teams how to design and implement improved process before investing more resources in a wasteful process.

Then, make the decision on whether the plan of action to correct is adding resources, improving processes or reducing expectations.

7. Do you get credit for the good results that you produce?

Getting an honest answer here is challenging. At the root of this question is an employee admitting that he has need for recognition which some people may be reluctant to admit. Remember that "credit" is both praise/recognition for good results as well as compensation for the value that the employee adds. You may need to explain that you know this is difficult to talk about, but that you also know from your own experience that not feeling appreciated has an impact on motivation and performance. Over time, experience may teach you that you need to modify this question. Alternatives might be, "do you feel that your contributions are appreciated?" or "do you feel valued?" or "are there steps I could take that would make you feel more valued?" Another question might be, "do you feel that your compensation and benefits are fair given your contributions?"

As stated previously, giving feedback on every work product is the best guarantee that you will get a "yes" on the feedback and credit questions.

Like the other questions, a "no" or "sometimes" should prompt a specific plan of action to get to "yes."

3. Evaluating Performance

You know by now that I am not a fan of the traditional annual evaluation process. It rarely adds value and worse, can cause damage. Evaluations tend to be one-way conversations with the manager sitting as judge and jury. This may be the only conversation managers have with employees and it serves to undermine effectiveness in fulfilling the role of reaching employee potential. It impedes open, honest, two-way communication and the building of relationship.

Evaluations usually entail placing numerical scores on vague questions intended to apply to every job. The judgements are largely subjective and don't lead to an effective game plan for improved performance. Everyone dreads them. Both supervisor and employee enter them with anxiety.

You have to ask, "what is the purpose of this exercise?" If it is to improve performance, it is underperforming. A 2020 Gallup report[5] on feedback to millennials found that only 17% reported that feedback helped them "learn, grow and do their jobs better." If the purpose is to determine who should get bonuses, it leads to the view

---

5 Gallup – "What 'Meaningful Feedback' Means to Millennials", Adam Hickman, Workplace, Jan. 29, 2020

that such decisions are arbitrary. If it is to improve relationships, who are we kidding? So, what is the utility?

Even a process involving the employee completing a self-evaluation and then comparing the scores with the supervisor is flawed. That's because the questions are too general and employees try to figure out how to game it rather than having honest discussion.

I say replace this practice with more frequent conversations around the 7 Questions and separate the conversation from decisions on compensation. The conversations should focus on how the manager can truly add value. Then, measure the performance and have this the basis for changes in compensation.

Numerous clients have replaced the traditional annual evaluation and consideration of compensation with a conversation using the 7 Questions. This one change shifted the organizational culture improving employee engagement while saving the management team hours of time. Once anxious and negative about evaluations, employees welcomed the conversations and looked forward to an opportunity to build relationships with their manager and add value in their work. Both managers and employees report a great sigh of relief. Supervision, performance and morale improved.

4. Assuring Fairness

Whether the "contract" between employee and organization is deemed to be fair impacts motivation to contribute more and to reach potential. The 7 Questions may reveal that you have done all that you should in supporting good performance but the employee still feels taken advantage of. Lack of fairness may impact all the areas covered by the 7 Questions, namely, expectations, standards, feedback, authority and resources needed, credit for results. If contributions are not fairly valued, then motivation declines.

For lack of fairness, the action plan should address how to get to fairness. Adjust compensation? Adjust distribution of work? Modify expectations? Hold others accountable for support? Confront underperformers? Elevate recognition? Increase feedback?

5. Determining the Real Why for Underperformance

Let's put aside the matter of a poor hiring decision. The 7Q's and improved management likely will not overcome the problem of hiring someone without the aptitude to succeed. Rather than drag both of you through a long slog that usually doesn't end well, cut both of your losses early and help your employee to find a better fit for motivations and talents, either within or outside the organization.

To solve the problem of underperformance, you need to determine the cause of that underperformance and who owns the solution. There are three potential factors that may be in play:

A. Can't Do – requisite skills or experience or clarity of direction or support are lacking

B. Won't Do – has proven skills but is currently choosing not to perform

C. Can't Do or Won't Do Sourced in Low Confidence – This could be someone terrified of speaking before groups, unable to confront an employee about poor performance, or someone fearful of making a mistake. Perhaps there is fear of reaction if not done exactly right. In the end, the employee simply won't try. In the 7 Questions conversation, you will be discussing performance on all the areas for which an employee is accountable to perform. Several of these causal factors may be in play. The supervisor and employee actions to correct performance will be determined by which of these causal factors explain failure to perform at full potential.

Let's explore each causal factor:

A. Can't Do

Unclear/conflicting direction or priorities, unclear standards for performance, lack of knowledge or skill, lack of feedback on results or unrealistic expectations due to lack of authority, lack of cooperation, and lack of resources are the culprits here. In each case, actions by the manager should be sufficient to fill in the gaps. Identify the missing items and then develop action steps to fill them.

B. Won't Do

In essence, the employee chooses to not perform at times despite past performance demonstrating he can do so or your best efforts to get "yes" responses to all the Questions. Finding the real why for this choice is challenging. The next chapter deals in depth with diagnosing and correcting the Won't Do's.

Responsibility to correct Won't Do problems are owned by the employee because ultimately, the individual has to choose to put his skills/experience to work and to perform. But you can have real influence on that choice. Remember Gena? She chose not to perform because she felt no one cared whether she performed or not. Remember Matt, the director of IT? He gave up because expectations of him were not doable. Remember Dave at Interior Air? He chose to not take on more responsibilities because he felt he was not given sufficient credit for his current performance.

In each case, a failing by the manager contributed to the employee's choice to not perform.

In other instances, the problem may be sourced outside of work. Addiction, mental health issues, financial problems, marital problems, and family woes all can sap the will to work.

There are two tendencies by managers that undermine effectiveness. The first is to falsely question or blame oneself for employee non-performance and therefore not take corrective action. The second is to falsely label or blame the employee as a Won't Do (such was the case with Gena for twenty-five years) when the real cause lies with lapses in management, in essence justifying not confronting the problem. Finding the real "why" is often messy, unpleasant to hear and requires persistence. But to not get there is to abandon your responsibility to get the most from all who work with you.

C. Can't Do Due to Low Confidence in Self or Manager
There may be primal fear of going it alone, fear of confronting team members or you may have given the message that you don't believe the employee will do it right. Feeling as if failure and shame or pain is inevitable means the individual can't get himself to do it on his own.

Consider a child that refuses to ride a bike without training wheels. The skill is there but the fear of a falling is overwhelming. Keeping your hands on her shoulders to prevent a fall might help here before letting go. Say an employee does well making presentations to small groups but is frozen in fear at the thought of facing 100 or more. Agreeing to do a joint presentation might overcome this block. Low self-confidence should be recognized as a Can't Do as the employee has intention to perform.

Can't Do due to low confidence of the manager can be trickier to uncover. I have worked with many leaders who complain that their employees just don't perform. They can't count on them. This is a common perception. When someone is learning there is a heightened sense of evaluation. The person is looking for evidence of his success or failure. When a manager has low confidence in a subordinate, the subordinate responds accordingly typically avoiding judgement by avoiding new work. All confidence issues are influenceable through actions by the manager.

5. Defining a Course of Correction for the Underperforming Employee

The 7 Questions are a checklist of the deliverables that managers are responsible to produce. A "no", "sometimes" or "usually" response to any question indicates there is more you can do to bring about better performance. You can then dialogue on what steps each of you can take to close the performance gap. If the "no" response is to a question doesn't explain the poor performance, then there must be another "why." You need to continue dialogue until the "real why" is found.

A manager I was coaching was disappointed by the lack of attention to detail in his subordinate's work. Customers continued to complain about it. He made several attempts to call attention to the problem and each time received a pledge of correction. In the manager's mind, both "expectations" and "standards" were clear (although he was making an assumption here rather than getting a "yes" to both questions), so now the question was "why is this continuing?" Was the employee unhappy, feeling unappreciated or feeling that his "contract" with the employer was unfair? Were there problems outside of work or a challenging medical issue? You can only find the truth by continuing to ask questions until it is revealed.

The proper course of action in response to "no's" is a step-by-step action plan for the manager to deliver what is needed to get to "yes" and the employee to step up performance. It becomes a revision to the "contract" with the employee.

In the next chapter, we will deal with "Won't Do" employees in some detail but for now, a word of caution with regard to defining a plan of action. "Won't Do's" may seek to continue forever the "game" of making you responsible for their choice to not perform. You may find yourself dealing with justifications that have no resolution, statements that are generalities without any real actionable data. The game they are playing is to not be found out. Ultimately, you have to call a halt to the game, indicate that you have done all you can, counsel them about making another career choice or conferring with HR if they feel they have been harassed.

I say this because I have often found that managers struggle to hold employees responsible for substandard performance. Some just struggle to sit in judgment of others. They don't want to be labeled as judgmental or they are not feeling so great about their own performance. Others rationalize that we are all human and struggle with life. It is common to get hung up on, "Is there something more that I should have done?" As long as that question is in play, the poor performance continues on. Overlooked is the impact on the rest of the team of the "game" continuing on.

The 7 Questions are intended to give you certainty as to the cause and cure for gaps in performance. To get to that certainty, try following the conversation outline in Appendix 3:

Meet with the employee and begin by detailing those account-abilities being performed well and those that are sub-standard. If you have not talked about the individual's level of performance before, then apologize for not having done so. Be as specific as possible (task, event and date what exactly was above and not up to standard) in your feedback.

If the employee gets defensive or wants to get into an explanation of the "why's" of the poor performance, ask the employee to hold off because you will be asking for that information in a moment (i.e., the 7 Questions are designed to pinpoint the "why's"). Then, explain that you want to identify what is contributing to poor performance and develop a plan for correction. State that you will be employing a series of questions to try and identify what needs to be corrected. Explain that what you are seeking is one or more "no" responses to help you determine what may be missing.

Then, go through the 7 Questions. If you get a "no" or a "well, I guess so," then ask for specifics as to what could have been provided by you that would have made a difference. Use the suggested clarifying questions to get to a level of specificity needed to develop an action plan. Ask the Questions in general or you can ask them about performance on each accountability.

Beware of the employee who speaks in generalities. You may hear, "Well, everybody is confused," or "I'm just doing what everyone else does," or "We all have questions," etc. These statements are attempts to avoid accountability. In short, they are intended to keep you pondering that question, "What else could I have done to prevent this?"

If you insist on specifics, the employee may go into guilt or shame and take on the characteristics of a victim in an effort to ward off you uncovering the true cause. Say that shame will do nothing to improve the performance. What is done is done. The question now is where we go from here. The employee may even attempt to build you up as part of this shameful response with statements about how understanding and patient you have been and so on. Again, this may be a tactic to gain your leniency and allow the employee avoid responsibility.

Insist on going through the 7 Questions as a check to assure that something has not been missed in supporting good performance. Document the employee responses. It is important to keep detailed notes of your conversations to provide a record for you and the employee. Detailed notes will 1) prepare you should you later determine to terminate the employee and need a clear case for HR and 2) protect you should the employee file a grievance in an attempt to prolong the game and confound you further.

Obviously, if there are specific needs identified as you go through the Questions, define detailed action steps and commit to deliver them on a timetable detailed in an action plan.

Regardless of what form of help the employee may need, a firm and tightly managed plan of action spelling out your future actions and holding the employee accountable for performance milestones should be put in place.

Remember, when the root causes are within the domain of the workplace, they likely will surface in the form of a "no" response to one of the 7 Questions. Exceptions to this might be factors, such as perceived harassment or lack of cooperation from fellow employees or the fact that methods imposed thru existing processes are wasteful and prevent meeting performance expectations. In both these cases, further investigation is needed to determine if the alleged root cause conditions must be remedied or whether these causes have been put forth to deflect responsibility.

Upon further investigation, if the root cause is the responsibility of the employee, then a management course of action that involves more support absolves the employee of responsibility for the poor performance. The manager is taking responsibility for that failure and continues to tilt at windmills trying to find a magic formula to get the employee back on track.

Root causes that are likely the responsibility of the employee might include the following: lack of dependable childcare, problems with spouse, inability to cooperate with co-workers, substance abuse, car problems, public transportation problems, medical issues and family problems.

Dealing with issues that aren't the responsibility of the manager is the subject of the next chapter. For now, remember that no matter the cause of underperformance, it should be confronted early, the root causes determined and a plan of action for correction involving commitments by both manager and employee should be defined and executed.

6. Increasing Employee Engagement

Gallup defines engaged employees as "those who are involved in, enthusiastic about and committed to their work and workplace." A widely used survey to measure engagement is the Gallup Q12Survey. It measures the following:

- Clarity of expectations
- Adequacy of resources
- Opportunity to be your best
- Recognition of work
- Supervisor care for individual
- Encouragement of development
- Consideration of employee opinion
- Importance of mission/purpose to employee
- Friendship at work
- Feedback on progress
- Opportunity to learn and grow

Recent research by Gallup and others have found the following:

- Engagement leads to a 20-30% reduction in turnover and increase in profits
- Engaged employees outperform their competition by as much as 202% (Gallup 2017)
- 35% of employees are engaged, 13% are disengaged and the majority are potentially positively influenced by good management practice
- Gallup research found that 70% of the variance in employee engagement scores were attributable to managers

There is little in the literature to guide managers on how to increase engagement. Organizations increasingly employ engagement software to gauge level of engagement rather than hold their managers accountable to 1) measure this on a one-on-one basis and 2) take effective action to raise it. It is left to the organization as a whole or the HR department and raising engagement scores remains elusive.

Engagement is about relationship; it is about both sides caring about the other. And relationship is built on the frequency and depth of communication. The 7Questions align with the dynamics of engagement and are measuring the effectiveness of managers. Asking all managers to employ the 7Questions puts responsibility for engagement squarely where it belongs, with each manager. Rather than asking whether the organization is delivering on engagement, the manager is asking each employee about his or her own success with engagement and then developing an action plan for improvement.

Frequency of Communication

Increasingly management advice recommends bi-weekly, ideally weekly, one-on-one conversations between manager and employees using a set of questions to gauge level of engagement.

Ken Blanchard recently shared with me a story involving his wife, Margie, working with a chain of fast-food restaurants that were experiencing turnover in excess of 100%. She learned there was one manager overseeing two restaurants that experienced only 20% turnover and sought him out to find out why. The manager revealed his practice of conducting weekly fifteen to thirty-minute one-on-one meetings with each employee in which the employee sets the agenda. The Ken Blanchard Companies now employ that practice and report great improvements in relationships with employees. The employee owns the time and can use it for whatever they wish.

I would recommend periodically revisiting the 7Questions in such meetings. The employee may not choose to discuss the

Questions but the manager should check-in to be assure fulfilling what employees need to remain engaged.

Putting the Questions to Work: Key Points

1. The five uses of the 7 Questions include improving onboarding, improving management practice, evaluating performance, assuring fairness and engagement and determining the proper course of action for an underperforming employee.

2. Onboarding is usually under-prioritized and resourced but is vital to getting early successes and retaining employees. It requires good planning and prioritization by the manager.

3. The 7 Questions are a checklist for success in on boarding and ongoing management practice.

4. A structured conversation around the 7 Questions should replace the annual evaluation process in most organizations. Separate the performance discussion from discussion of compensation.

5. Finding the root cause of underperformance is challenging. The 7 Questions begin that investigation but persistence is often needed. Beware of employee strategies to avoid specifics.

6. Lack of confidence may impede an employee taking independent action. This is normally correctable with good management practice.

7. Do not define a course of correction without certainty as to the root cause.

8. Use the 7 Questions to avoid the trap of assuming you are somehow at fault for poor performance and not taking action to correct it.

9. The 7 Questions operationalize the responsibility of managers to engage employees. Answers to the Questions and dialogue about what else employees need serve as an action plan for raising engagement.

10. Weekly or bi-weekly brief one-on-one meetings to check-in and maintain relationship is best practice. No less than every 90 -days, such meetings should include revisiting the 7 Questions to assure that conditions for employee success are being maintained.

9.

Identifying and Handling
the "Won't Do" Employee

Do not make the mistake of assuming that an underperformance is a "Won't Do" problem. Remember the story of Gena? Yes, she was choosing to not perform, i.e. Won't Do, but it was because her work was not appreciated. Had the 7 Questions been employed, the root cause would have become clear and the situation could have been corrected. Instead, she was labeled, management absolved themselves of responsibility and put her on the shelf for two decades. You have to do the hard work to find the truth.

Identifying a Won't Do Situation

If you have gotten a "yes" to all the Questions, but performance isn't meeting expectations, or you are getting generalities as to why the response is "no," then you may have a Won't Do situation. The challenge is to determine whether you got false "yes" responses out of employee fear to be honest or whether the employee is blocking efforts to uncover the truth and trying to end this conversation.

Let's review the symptoms of a Won't Do situation:

- Employee is not meeting standards. There is lots of apparent activity but no tangible results from his work.

- Employee appears manic, i.e., always busy, engaged, opinionated, at the center of it all. This hides the lack of real productivity.

- Employee is somewhat out of control in life. This is evidenced by chronically being late, showing poor money management (i.e. difficulty in managing personal finances and debt), inefficiency and dispersed energy (i.e., chronically jumping from one task to another rather frantically without gaining completion on those tasks).

- When asked about "why" or what the problem may be, the employee speaks in generalities, e.g., "everyone thinks....". The person is unable to identify the who, because the employee's statements are false and simply sow confusion.

- Teams with Won't Do employees underperform, have low morale, high number of sick days and high turnover.

- Teams are unable to problem solve. No solution involving a straight line will be created or executed. A new supposed wrinkle is always introduced to derail efforts to find and handle the truth.

The source of these symptoms is the Won't Do employee's fear of being controlled and being found out. The individual shows up as your most loyal, informed, engaged and motivated employee but neither the person nor his team is producing. This is what makes this employee so difficult to spot and prevents managers from handling the situation, e.g. "It can't be Bob, he is my best employee." Managers sit in a stew of self-doubt and performance suffers.

Having gone thru the 7 Questions without identifying the cause of underperformance, the conversation then might continue as follows:

Manager: I appreciate your honesty in answering the questions. What concerns me is that having gotten a "yes" to all the questions (or no specifics as to what else you need to do to get to a "yes"); I am at a loss as to what I can do to improve your performance. I want to be clear that at this point, your performance is not up to standard or what is needed from your position. The specifics of where you are failing are..................... Do you have any questions about that? Have we missed anything that I could have done to prevent the sub-standard performance you have contributed as of late?

Employee: Really, I don't know.

Manager: Are you reluctant to share with me where I may not be meeting my responsibilities to you or any factors outside of work that explain what's going on?

Employee: Well, yes, ...

Manager: Well, only you can solve these conditions outside of work. I am happy to give you time off to handle them or to support your getting any help that you may need, but we can't continue to have these conditions impact the performance we are experiencing. I would like to suggest that getting the work part of your life back on track may help you face and handle the conditions outside of work.

Key is getting the employee to understand that 1) performance is not meeting the requirements of the job (and possibly not up to previous performance) and 2) the need to take responsibility for the choice not to meet expectations. Without these two shifts, a workable plan to improve performance is not attainable. In short, the employee must self-identify as a Won't Do for the situation to be resolved.

Those Who Choose to Fail

Employees who don't perform despite taking all the steps outlined in previous chapters fall into two categories: 1) those who can't face the personal issues which only they can fix and 2) those whose previous experiences have taught them that the only survival strategy at work is to create chaos around them in order to avoid accountability and punishing control. There is also a smaller third category involving those lacking the confidence to take on a new challenge or to move on to acting independently on a task with which you have provided coaching. This third category can be addressed using the 7 Questions and development of a sound action plan to move them forward. Now, let's address the two main groups for whom the 7 Questions and action plan to improve supervision, training and coaching won't do the trick.

1. *Those with Personal Issues*

Issues include dealing with divorce, loss of loved ones, chronic health issues, addiction issues, etc. The inability to face these issues will bleed into their work with resulting loss of motivation, inability to focus, inability to be honest with themselves or others. This may be temporary, but it needs to be confronted early by the manager.

The proper strategy can best be described as "tough love." It combines compassion and accountability based on understanding that the employees need something to stabilize their life. Getting work performance back on track can be that opportunity. Ultimately, the employee must make the choice to change. Employing the 7 Questions can lead to the realization that such a choice is needed.

These situations are indeed very challenging. Employees with personal issues often can't afford to lose their job or add to their existing problems. But they know, on some deeper level, that they are not performing and don't feel good about it. Employing "tough love" to get them feeling good about performance will strengthen them and provide a foundation from which they can better face the other issues in their lives.

2. *Those Creating Chaos*

It is this second category that can be particularly troublesome for managers. It is because these individuals are a mystery clouded in false enthusiasm and non-productive hyper-activity. They are tough to spot and to confront.

An Exemplifying Story: I first came across this more than two decades ago while working with an insurance group. The group had been in chaos for some time but couldn't figure out why or find a solution.

I noticed as we went through the day that the most vocal member of the group kept challenging my questions. She was speaking for others and kept preventing the group from getting consensus on "what is." Whenever the discussion came to a specific point, she moved back to a generality or offered an exception to what was being said. Consequently, the source of problems could never be identified. Because she had been with the company the longest, she kept bringing up history with which others were not familiar. She was using information, hidden from others in the group, to divert the group from a solution. The group deferred to her because in the culture of the organization, she owned the history, experience and the "I am committed" card. No one would challenge her.

I was experiencing the frustration that the group had been experiencing. As the day went on, I began to push back to ask for specifics. What data? Why specifically would this not work? She began to back down. The atmosphere in the room grew dark, indeed. The group became anxious as they perceived that the "mother hen" was under attack. As the day ended, it was clear that only one of us, i.e., she or me, would survive the next day.

Well, it turned out that she arrived at work about an hour early the next day. She must have thought about it all night and on the drive. I think she saw the handwriting on the wall that her game was going to be up if I continued my line of questioning in front of the group. Not wanting to be exposed, she chose to write a letter of resignation and put it on the director's desk before the session began.

Initially, the group was in shock and dismay. They could not see how they could go on without her as they went to her for all the answers. Well, it turns out they not only did fine without her, they prospered. After getting through all the emotions for the first hour or so, the group effectively problem solved throughout the course of the day and then prospered from that point forward.

I had not seen this phenomenon before but have seen it several times since. The ability of such individuals to keep co-workers and a manager wrapped around the axle is something to behold. Because of the created confusion, the manager can't get to a solution. It is like driving in a blinding fog. You just can't see clearly enough to proceed. So, you don't.

It has been my experience that this manic behavior to avoid being found is sourced in a history of failure. Individuals may have been placed in positions for which they were not qualified and had to fake it or they were victims of bad control by a previous manager. The victims of bad control end up in confusion and enter into a game of avoid the punisher. Their real fear is that they cannot perform and therefore develop sophisticated strategies to hide that inability. Rather than respond "no" to the 7 Questions and relying on help from their manager, they sow confusion.

An Analogy

If you are attempting to train someone who has experienced nothing but losses in her education to date, you will have a very hard time being successful. Losses in education arise from the embarrassment of not having the answer when called on by the teacher, getting low test scores, being held back a grade, not getting into gifted and talented programs, or comparing oneself to other students and concluding inferiority.

Such students will avoid the training (out sick, family emergency, schedule conflicts) in order to avoid another loss. Or they will attend the training but not offer questions. Instead, they will pretend that they are getting it and appear to be the model student. Rather than focusing on learning the material, they are focusing on avoiding attention of the punisher, in this case the teacher. They will summarize and state back what the teacher has said, so they appear to be a model student without ever really internalizing the information or thinking about how it might apply to their job/life. Therefore, they never learn it. They are just the teacher's pet, but at the end of the day they cannot and will not apply the learning because they simply have not learned it. Rather than getting smarter, the student falls further behind. Not wanting to continue to experience losses, they either avoid education or find ways to pretend they are getting it. It's a coping mechanism. Thus, they appear to be something they are not.

A similar pattern exists with some employees. They appear to be saying and doing all the right things, but when you examine their results, they don't meet standards. These employees appear energetic, busy and committed. They speak up at meetings and are often looked up to by others. They are the informal opinion leaders. But, if you carefully examine the statistics of their work, they are not getting results. There are always explanations for these lapses. They create a culture of reasons or excuses vs. results. Because they appear to be so committed, managers do not confront them. The excuses and apologies for the errors are accepted and the non-performance continues.

As in the education analogy, the source of this is previous losses. Either because of honest mistakes or bad supervision, the employee has been brutalized. They are convinced that they cannot get it right, so the strategy they employ is the avoidance of responsibility. They may not be conscious of it, but they don't believe they can succeed. So, it becomes about looking good rather than doing good.

An Important Distinction

I want to distinguish between those creating chaos from those who don't want the training wheels taken off, i.e., those who don't want to act independently on a responsibility.

For both, the root cause may be that they have been punished for mistakes in the past. The employee who lacks confidence is much easier to handle than the employee who has experienced so much loss. Those lacking confidence can be rehabilitated, by encouragement and the equivalent of a hand on the shoulder much like when the child takes his first ride without the training wheels. That is, you will break the fall or prevent serious consequences from a mistake.

The Handling

Handling those seeking to create chaos and avoid accountability is challenging. Employ the 7 Questions but you will likely never get a "yes" to all 7 Questions if they know in the end, that the judgment will be that the fault lies with them.

People in this group seek to maintain confusion. Hence, they are never quite clear and that lack of clarity, which is your responsibility, is offered as the cause for the substandard performance. They will avoid ascribing the lack of clarity to something you have failed to do (too easily corrected). Instead, you may hear something like:

- *Well, I thought that _____ (likely another employee or department) was responsible for that."*
- *" _____ communicated to me that we should wait before proceeding."*
- *" _____ said they wanted to handle it."*
- *"That directive was not clear to me and I wasn't sure who was responsible."*

The blanks will be filled either by a generality or an unidentifiable group. There will be an avoidance of naming an individual because it would be too easy to simply ask that individual and learn that no such communication ever occurred.

So, when employing the 7 Questions, you will need to be persistent in nailing down just exactly what the source of the confusion was, who said what, etc. If not, the process of you continuing to fill in the imagined gaps in your management in pursuit of a "yes" response will go on forever. You will be tilting at windmills.

You may be tempted to excuse the poor performance because of the seeming exuberance and commitment to work. This is the trap that managers find difficult to escape. The 7 Questions are designed to penetrate the camouflage and reveal to all that the solution lies with the employee and not the supervisor.

How to Handle Those Who Choose to Not Perform

Here's a list of steps that will help you handle the "Won't Do" employees:

1. Confront the situation as early as possible. That may seem obvious and simple but given that this person may well show up as your most loyal team member, it can be challenging. You have to focus on the data of actual results and not the behavior or spoken word.

2. Begin the discussion with, *"I have noticed that things aren't going well lately and I want to get this sorted out. To do this I want to go through a checklist of my responsibilities to provide the clarity and support you need to be successful. I want to be certain and specific as to what I need to do to get this turned around."* This will likely be met with shock at the news that it is not going well. There will be a challenge to provide data on specifics on the non-performance. Be prepared to deliver those specifics.

3. There may very well be an emotional outburst based on the person's loyalty and commitment to you. The employee will feel betrayed that you have judged the person for not performing and complain that you have unfairly withheld feedback. You will need to get through that outburst and respond with the specifics on what was not done or not done well. Stress that this is about doing well moving ahead rather than relitigating the past.

4. Each specific may then be challenged. You will need to reinforce the employee's responsibility for a given goal or task because confusion about that will be used as a defense.

You will need to adjudicate what is lack of information and what is the avoidance of responsibility for results.

5. If you decide that, in fact, you were not clear and that this contributed significantly to the non-performance, provide whatever information/training/direction is needed to get to a "yes" in an action plan.

6. Do not delay putting the employee on a very tight watch for task completions. State that you want to start fresh while addressing whatever contributed to the lack of clarity in the past. Go to a one-week task list that is tightly defined.

7. Meet at the end of each week and go over the results. You will quickly see either a) a pattern of improved performance or b) continued avoidance of responsibility for poor results.

8. If you are witnessing avoidance, then quickly communicate that it is your judgment that the employee is choosing to fail. There will be protest, again about the lack of clarity of expectations, standards and the like. Insist upon specifics and verify their truth before assuming that the poor performance is somehow your responsibility.

9. This game can go on forever if you let it. Ask yourself what responsibility is the employee taking his or herself to gain clarity either from you or from co-workers. Since managers tend to beat themselves up for the non-performance, employees in this category can be very successful in masking the truth and having these games go on forever.

10. If the employee choses to address the performance lapses, elements of an action plan might include a formal warning, weekly performance targets, weekly check-in on whether

targets are met and clarity that failure to meet those targets will result in termination.

Weekly performance targets should address areas where performance has been lacking. They could include attendance, due dates on assignments, responsiveness to communications or stepped-up productivity, such as sales calls or patients seen.

11. If the employee choses to not take responsibility, then advise the person to seek a position with another company and get a fresh start as you have exhausted potential remedies. If the person doesn't take that advice, again put the employee on the tight performance plan but forewarn the person that you don't believe this is going to end well. If the employee does not meet the goals in the performance plan, then move forward on a progressive discipline plan as defined by your personnel policies or in consultation with the HR department. But remember, you have already done all that you can as a manager to support the employee at this point and he is avoiding responsibility for a choice to perform which only he can make.

A Final Word on Those Choosing to Fail

As a final point here, I would note that coming to a judgment that someone is willfully (consciously or unconsciously) creating chaos to avoid accountability may fly in the face of your core beliefs. You simply can't get yourself to judge someone that harshly. But, having been played by such individuals and seeing other managers suffer the same has convinced me that this phenomenon exists. My advice would be to separate your judgment of performance from judgment of the individual. The poor performance and employee responsibility for it may be truth. State your judgement and ask if that is who the individual wants to be. You're calling a halt to the game that you both are playing, which serves both of you in the long run. It enables better choices. The question is, with the truth on the table, what choice do they wish to make?

Identifying and Handling the "Won't Do" Employee — Key Points

1. Avoid labeling underperformers as Won't Do until you have diagnosed why as the source may indeed be manager underperformance.

2. Use the 7 Questions to confirm that you have done all that you can to support success to gain certainty that you need to confront what is the employee's choice to not perform

3. True Won't Do's are difficult to spot and often appear as highly engaged and busy.

4. Won't Do's won't be solved until the employee has taken responsibility

5. Won't Do's sourced in issues outside of work need "tough love," i.e., heightened accountability with support to handle their issues.

6. The key is to get the employee to make the choice to take responsibility for the non-performance or continue the game of avoidance. Make clear that continuing the avoidance game will not end well.

7. Action plans should be tightly framed with weekly accountabilities and check-in on performance with the threat of more serious actions if below standard performance persists.

10.

Troubleshooting

Other factors may impact getting to the truth and being able to develop an action plan to improve performance.

The following are some troubleshooting tips:

A. The "Yes Man"

There will be a tendency for employees to answer "yes" to the questions, in order not to complain about or upset the manager. Honest dialogue with authority figures is not something that employees have a lot of experience in. The more damaged by previous authority figures or the more insecure, the more likely this scenario will happen.

Contributing to a false "yes" may be not wanting to be a complainer, believing that the corporate culture rewards the tough who just find a way to "get 'er done" despite obstacles, or sensing that the manager may punish the employee if given the truth.

If you sense discomfort as you ask the questions, emphasize the concept of partnering for performance. Make clear that you use the Questions to identify the part each of you can play in reaching the employee's full potential and job satisfaction. Getting all "yes" responses means you have no opportunity to add value which is your intent.

Ask that in considering each question, if the answer is "yes," but it could have gone better or come sooner and should for the next employee, then answer with "no" or "somewhat," and then define how to improve.

Asking for advice on how you can get the next person in that position towards success may be a way to bypass the reluctance of the employee from being honest about their experience. The employee may find offering advice about the future easier than "complaining" about the past.

Examples: Could onboarding have been improved? Is leadership practice sending a signal on what is important that is different than what was understood from the job description? Is leadership practice actually eroding the authority of the employee by second-guessing decisions or penalizing mistakes?

Even if the employee answers "yes," there is value in asking the additional questions detailed in each chapter to gain greater understanding.

Lastly, if you get all "yes" responses but sense that you are not getting the truth, consider taking a break and ask the employee to give it further thought as you wish to find ways to improve. Schedule a meeting in a few days hence and see if you get different responses.

B. Those Lacking Motivation

Partnerships require two. You cannot will someone to their full potential; the person has to want to get there. Your employee "partner" must share the goal of realizing potential or career advancement. The 7 Questions method assumes motivation because that will be true for the majority of those you engage with. But there are those who are simply content where they are in their career and in their performance level. As long as standards are being met, you have little leverage to gain improvement. State that you see the potential for career advancement and should the employee choose to want to, that you will aid them. Then, continue to affirm that they are meeting standards in future meetings and check to see if their ambition has shifted.

There may be instances in which the employee just seeks to get by. The job is not that important or the person is longer engaged in the purpose and vision of the organization. He knows his performance is not poor enough to get terminated and he doesn't rise to a call to reach his potential. The challenge here is the impact of such attitudes on co-workers. The one point of leverage that you have is a future need for a reference. Encourage the person to find what does motivate him as being unmotivated at work is a terrible way to spend the majority of one's waking hours. That is, encourage the person to move on and get a fresh start potentially but to go out performing well. Communicate that you want to honestly endorse the employee for a future position but can't do so at the moment.

C. Those Inappropriately Elevated to Management

Commonly, those with the best technical skills are promoted to management. The underlying belief is that somehow their expertise will serve as an example or rub off on others and thereby performance of their teams will improve. But the skills, values and priorities for effective management are a real shift from technical work. Without an aptitude to make this shift and training on how to manage, new managers often underperform. These managers are frustrated by their subordinates, lack the will to hold subordinates accountable, lack patience to invest time in employee development and continue to do technical work to escape having to confront performance problems.

An underlying cause here is the ceiling on compensation for technical work extant in most companies. Moving ahead means having to manage others. Some firms overcome this by creating positions for "masters" in technical skills who become trainers or mentors but have no management responsibility. Organizations that don't establish such positions tend to promote technical high performers into management work for which they are not suited.

If you are managing another manager and sense this person is not interested in doing management work, ask questions to gain clarity on this. Be clear about the person's underperformance and use the 7 Questions and others to diagnose whether it is a problem of lack of training/coaching or lack of motivation/sense of purpose to manage, i.e. develop others. If it is the latter, indicate that this will not end well if current conditions continue. Ask honestly whether a return to technical work is not the best fit going forward and then develop an action plan based on your findings.

D. The Disgruntled

A variation of the Won't Do employee is one justifying non-performance or compliance on the grounds that the direction, policies, practices of the organization are not correct. They Won't Do it because it is not the best or right way. They may even be performing well in terms of production but they are corrosive to team morale. This is similar to the employee who has lost motivation.

Before facing this situation, ask yourself whether the employee point of view has merit and has been considered. If not, then pledge to do so and coach the employee to correct performance for the moment. Follow-up to inform the individual when and how his ideas have been considered.

For cases where displeasure is used to justify low performance, the non-performance has to be confronted. State that you welcome receiving actual data (vs. opinion) making the case for changes in direction, policy and the like. However, the displeasure cannot justify not performing. The "know it all" may try to make you wrong for supporting wrong-headed practices and put you on the defensive. These are all tactics to avoid accountability, follow or enforce policy and you need to rise to the occasion and call it for what it is. After all, when the person becomes a CEO based on his performance, then he can call the shots.

Troubleshooting — Key Points

1. Consider that "yes" responses may be false, arising out of fear. Make clear that "no's" create opportunity for you to add value. Use follow-up questions if you sense a false "yes." Consider re-scheduling after further consideration by employee.

2. Accept with someone performing at standard but lacking motivation to move forward in his or her career at this time. Make certain that there is not a lack of motivation impacting other employees.

3. Correcting situations where technical peak performers have been elevated to management without aptitude or training may not be doable. Create pathways for technical high performers to get ahead without taking on management responsibility if it simply is not to their liking or strength.

4. Those disgruntled who believe that strategy, policy, methods etc. are wrong-headed need to be reminded that their input is welcomed but they are responsible to execute based on decisions made. Coach them to bring forth data to support their views and indicate a willingness to revisit decisions but don't allow being their disgruntled to justify below standard performance.

11.

Some Final Thoughts

As discussed in Chapter 3, most managers simply don't give management work enough time or attention, hence the "management gap" that Lewis Allen researched. The legendary CEO of ITT, Harold Gineen, referred to the same problem in his book *Managing*[6], when he wrote, "managers must manage."

Well, why the "gap", why don't they manage? Allen found that managers choose to do technical work if given a choice because that's their experience and proven expertise. It is what they know best, are certain they can do well, what gives them the greatest satisfaction and quickly produces results. They think that somehow their expertise will get instilled via osmosis. However, management requires an entirely different set of skills and the valuing of employee development. Often technical experts are thrust into it without the values, aptitude or training on those skills.

---

6 Gineen, H., Managing, Doubleday, 1984

Management work is messy. Good outcomes are less tangible, take a long time to produce and involve dealing with people which is not straight forward or predictable.

Managers often question their performance. Their self-doubt renders them incapable of effectively confronting the underperforming employee. The 7 Questions, in part, serve as a report card on your performance. By building your certainty, the ability to handle performance problems is raised. One of my goals is to end the agony of managers continuing to hold themselves responsible for employee choices to underperform.

My hope in writing this book is that I have helped you close your personal "management gap" and that the 7 Questions will make it easier for you to face, dialogue and plan with subordinates. I also hope that you can realize the immense satisfaction that can come from growing those who work for you. Despite the challenges of management work, doing it well can be the ultimate satisfaction and legacy.

As you look back on a career, undoubtedly promotions and reaching goals has been gratifying. But my take is that you will value most seeing those who work for you succeed. Their success may be the ultimate success for you. The relationships that build such success can become the most rewarding in life.

In the end, it is really all about relationships. Like our personal relationships, work relationships are best established and maintained through open, honest communication. We spend the bulk of our waking hours at work. The promise of a workplace can be to deliver pride, satisfaction and reward in what we do as a team. It should be more than what we do to support and earn time with family and other interests. Work can serve to energize us to give to family and community rather than the reverse.

The intent of the 7 Questions is to help you deliver on that promise and thereby enrich your own life.

Appendix 1

The Seven Questions

Supervisor:

Instructions: Please answer "yes" or "no" to each of the following questions. In considering your answer, look as to whether you are receiving the information from your supervisor vs. determining for yourself. If you are not sure of your answer, then answer "no."

1. Do you know what is expected of you? ☐Yes ☐No

2. Do you know what good performance looks like in your job as defined by your supervisor?☐Yes ☐No

3. Do you get feedback on the results that you produce? ☐Yes ☐No

4. Do you have sufficient authority to carry out your responsibilities? ☐Yes ☐No

5. Do you get timely decisions in the areas where you don't have authority? ☐Yes ☐No

6. Do you have the data, resources and support needed to meet what is expected of you? ☐Yes ☐No

7. Do you get credit for the good results that you produce? ☐Yes ☐No

Appendix 2

For Job Descriptions:

Sample Purposes

For Director of Sales - To create revenue to maintain future viability and growth.

For Information Technology - To establish and maintain information management systems that support productivity and effective decision-making within the company.

For HR - To assure that; a) the organization has sufficient staff to support effective operations, b) all persons employed or contracted by the company are well and properly placed in service, and each one's forward progress as a staff member is uninterrupted and c) management of personnel conforms to applicable state and federal laws/regulations.

Sample Products

For Director of Sales

- A well-trained, effective sales force

- Campaigns to generate interest in continuing to do business with our organization are designed and implemented
- Sales data on customers and prospective customers are maintained and understood by all staff
- Policies in place and followed to support effective sales function

For Information Technology

- Effective I.T. strategy defined and updated that maintains cutting edge position relative to competitors
- Hardware & software needs of the organization are addressed to ensure cost effective and efficient operations
- Policies and procedures established that maintain effective and efficient I.T. practices
- Staff literate in I.T. applications, so it does not hamper performance

For HR

- Budgeted positions filled with competent, qualified personnel
- New personnel understand company philosophy, principles, policies, benefits and expectations
- Employee records are maintained
- Performance management and compensation systems maintained.
- All benefits received by eligible employees
- Effective employee training and development program carried out

- All applicable laws and regulations are adhered to and personnel policies remain current
- Supervisors coached on handling personnel matters
- Employee grievances adjudicated
- Internal staff publication produced monthly

Sample Statistics

For Director of Sales

- Gross revenue scheduled
- Gross revenue profitability of jobs
- Opportunities lost

For Information Technology

- Computer down time, service interruptions
- Technical assistance work requests
- Trainings conducted

For HR

- Number of open positions
- Time to fill vacancies
- Grievances filed
- Number of trainings delivered

Appendix 3

Documentation of 7 Question Conversation

Date:

Employee:

Manager:

Current Performance and Performance Goals

Responsibility/Task	Current Performance Relative to Standards	New Performance Goal

Assessment of Causes of Current Performance

Question	Response per Responsibility	Possible Needs per Responsibility
1. Do you know what is expected of you?		
2. Do you know what good performance looks like in your job as defined by your supervisor?		

3. Do you get feedback on the results that you produce?		
4. Do you have sufficient authority to carry out your responsibilities?		
5. Do you get timely decisions in the areas where you don't have authority?		
6. Do you have the data, resources and support needed to meet with is expected of you?		
7. Do you get good credit for the good results that you produce?		

Action Plan for Improved Performance

Performance Goal	Action Steps	Responsible	Due

Manager:_____

Employee:_____

About the Author

William Dann spent thirteen years in management, including nine years as CEO. He launched his consulting business in 1981 with a passion for enabling organizations and individuals to reach their fullest potential. He also taught management at the graduate level for six years at Boston University.

His company, Professional Growth Systems LLC, has served more than 200 organizations in the U.S. and overseas using proprietary solutions developed by his team to accelerate performance using the least possible time and resources. Throughout his career, Bill has continued to focus on improving the methods that spark innovation while overcoming resistance to change. He has also served as a coach to numerous CEO's. In *Creating High Performers,* he details his own experiences learning how to develop those you work with and how to do it with certainty.

Bill maintains a blog and newsletters on management and governance.

Bill and his wife, Jenny, live in Anchorage, Alaska with son, Tyler and his family, including two grandchildren close by.

To subscribe to his newsletters and read his blog, visit
http://www.professionalgrowthsystems.com/
You can also connect with Bill on
LinkedIn https://www.linkedin.com/in/william-dann-4037b8/
or **Twitter** https://www.twitter.com/arcticwill